P9-ASG-757

THE ABDICATION
OF
EDWARD

DA
580
W45
1937

J. Lincoln White

THE ABDICATION OF

EDWARD VIII

*A Record with all
the Published Documents*

LONDON

GEORGE ROUTLEDGE & SONS, LTD.

BROADWAY HOUSE: 68–74 CARTER LANE, E.C.

1937

UNIVERSITY OF WINNIPEG
LIBRARY
DISCARDED
515 Portage Avenue
Winnipeg, Manitoba R3B 2E9

MADE AND PRINTED IN GREAT BRITAIN
AT GAINSBOROUGH PRESS, ST. ALBANS
BY FISHER, KNIGHT AND CO., LTD.

CONTENTS

ROYAL FAMILY TABLE OF SUCCESSION

KING EDWARD VII = Princess
b. 1841, acceded 1901, | Alexandra
d. 1910. | of Denmark,
m. 1863, d. 1925.

| Albert Victor, Duke of Clarence, b. 1864, d. 1892. | KING GEORGE V = Princess Mary of Teck, m. 1893. b. 1865, acceded 1910, d. 1936 | Alexander died in infancy. b. 1871. | Louise, Princess Royal, b. 1867. m. 1889, d. 1931. | = Duke of Fife, d. 1912. | Victoria, b. 1868, d. 1935. | Maud, b. 1869, m. 1896. | = Haakon VII, King of Norway. |

KING EDWARD VIII, b. 1894, acceded 1936; abdicated Dec. 11, 1936. | KING GEORGE VI, b. 1895; acceded Dec. 11, 1936. | = Lady Elizabeth Bowes-Lyon, m. 1923. | Henry, Duke of Gloucester, b. 1900. | = Lady Alice Christabel Scott, m. 1935. | George, Duke of Kent, b. 1902. | = Princess Marina of Greece, m. 1934. | John, b. 1905, d. 1919. | Mary, Princess Royal, b. 1897, m. 1922. | = Earl of Harewood.

Princess Elizabeth, b. 1926. | Princess Margaret Rose, b. 1930.

Prince Edward, b. 1935.

George Henry Viscount Lascelles, b. 1923. | Gerald David, b. 1924.

I have done the state some service, and they know it ;—
No more of that.—I pray you in your letters,
When you shall these unlucky deeds relate,
Speak of me as I am ; nothing extenuate,
Nor set down aught in malice : then must you speak
Of one that loved, not wisely, but too well.

OTHELLO

Chapter I

THE KING MEETS ROMANCE

In the chill, small, morning hours of December 12, 1936, the British destroyer, *Fury*, slipped out of Portsmouth harbour into the dark waters of the English Channel. Her destination was secret, but her departure was incident to the last act of a drama which for ten days had enthralled the world.

As she nosed her way south she was the cynosure still of the anxious millions who but a few hours before had heard the dignified beauty of a Monarch's love confession in his final speech to the peoples over whom he had reigned. A hushed world had listened to Britain's popular King renouncing Title, Estate and Empire for the sake of the woman he loved. The pathos of that moment had been heightened in the hearts of his people by the knowledge that the woman, too, was among the millions who heard his broadcast message.

And now the world, vicariously, watched. For the *Fury* was sailing into the future, bearing through the night one who, for a brief period a great King, was no longer a King. She was launching into the centuries the most romantic story of all time.

Simultaneously, the scene was closing on a crisis unprecedented in a thousand years of English history. Cabinet Ministers, Law Officers, Church Dignitaries, the King's Family and the Nation turned from the stress of Edward VIII's abdication to proclaim at three o'clock on the same day the accession of his brother Albert, Duke of York, as George VI.

The crisis, constitutional for the country, personal for the King, deeply emotional for all concerned, was over. A problem unparalleled in England's constitutional history had found solution in the King's sacrifice. The Monarch might marry whom he liked, but he could continue to reign only if his choice fell upon a woman whom his Ministers could accept as Queen.

Thus in one of the shortest and, while it lasted —three hundred and twenty-five days—one of the happiest reigns, did Edward VIII, King of Great Britain, Northern Ireland and the British Dominions Beyond the Seas, Defender of the Faith, and Emperor of India, step down from the throne of his fathers to become enshrined in an empire of romance where he will reign immortal so long as men are moved by the simple telling of a lover's tale.

During the few short days in which the drama rushed to its climax the crisis was one of expectation, conjecture and possibility rather than of fact. Captivated by the personal elements of the problem when it suddenly became known that the King wished to marry Mrs. Simpson, the public was confused rather than excited by the political aspects. Not until the King had himself determined upon the solution was it generally realized that he had never at any time challenged constitutional practice.

He had but obliged his Ministers to define more precisely their authority over the matrimonial affairs of the Crown. The public was anxiously expectant. Would the King, faced with the opposition of his Ministers to his marriage as King and their refusal to countenance a morganatic [1] marriage, stake wife and throne on an appeal to his unquestioned popularity with the mass of his people ?

Speculation as to the result, had such a challenge been made, may be a fit subject for politician and historian. The fact that it was not made and that the King faced the sorrowful alternative alone—separated from the influence of the woman he loved and withdrawn from public acclaim—not only obviated what might have become a serious dispute but rendered less difficult the unhappy task of his Ministers. And his personal regard in the public mind was greatly enhanced. It was conduct appropriate to his dignity as a Monarch. It was typical of his character as a Man.

For King Edward VIII will be remembered by the qualities which endeared him to his countrymen as a man rather than a monarch. He was

[1] MORGANATIC MARRIAGE : Marriage between persons of unequal rank, in which the inferior partner and the children of the marriage cannot enjoy the rank or inherit the property of the superior, though the children are legitimate. Frequent practice among Continental royalty.

esteemed for his simplicity, his straightforwardness, his love for sharing the common lot of his subjects and his unconcealed concern for the underdog. Throughout his life he rebelled against the tradition which sought to keep him aloof from the crowd. Always ready to forsake the sombre cares of State and become the embodiment of good fellowship, he was no less ready to make his protest on behalf of those, his fellows, who appeared to him the victims of a national injustice. His kingship might have provoked many a crisis less unexpected than the one which arose to deprive him of it.

Edward Albert Christian George Andrew Patrick David, named after his grandfather, his religion and the patron saints of the isles he was one day to rule, was born on June 23, 1894. He spent his boyhood in the shadow of a new age. He had scarcely been invested Prince of Wales at Caernarvon Castle in 1911 when the world began to exhibit all the portents of impending war. In the August of his twenty-first year the storm broke. Three months later he was in France where even the closest vigilance of his *aide-de-camp* failed to confine him to the quarters in which his superiors considered him safe. The story of his reckless escapades is scattered at random in the reminiscences of many comrades who encountered him at the front.

Back from the war, he bore among his father's subjects the comradeship, courage and sense of unity which the struggle had taught. During a decade of economic adaptation and social change he gathered stature among the people by his ready and apt response to the manifold problems of the national life. He went everywhere, met everybody. At home, in the Empire and abroad he earned the esteem and gratitude of high and low. Always he strove for equality among his fellows. His slogan, once stated, always implicit, on his tours of investigation was "No escort, no top-hats". Everywhere his was the human interest, the personal touch. He was warmly remembered in the wake of all his travels.

Throughout this period his life as a bachelor was determined for him by the aftermath of war as surely as it determined that two of his brothers and his sister should find partners among the commoners of England. A post-war Britain found that large tracts of the Empire needed composing, and the task fell to the young Prince. Visits to all parts of the Empire fell to his lot, long, exhausting journeys in India, Africa and the major Dominions. America called him the greatest commercial traveller in the world. Edward, Prince of Wales, worked as was expected of him, and the British Empire recovered from the blows it had received from war and post-war storms.

It would be hasty and unfair to blame Edward VIII for the tragedy which ultimately befell him. It is after all a simple story. As far back as 1920 Mrs. Bessie Wallis Wingfield Spencer first saw Edward, Prince of Wales, during one of his visits to America. There is no record that they met on that occasion, and it was not until 1931 that they became formally acquainted, and then under circumstances unimportant enough.

On a Sunday night in 1931, Mr. and Mrs. Benjamin Thaw remembered that they had a dinner engagement with Mr. and Mrs. Ernest Simpson. The Prince suggested they should telephone the unknown couple and invite them to Fort Belvedere for dinner. The Simpsons were delighted to accept the invitation. Later that evening the Prince found this young couple most charming. Followed other meetings, and the acquaintanceship ripened.

Mrs. Simpson proved to be a charming and fascinating woman. It was not unnatural that the Prince should seek her company. She moved in that emancipated "socialite" society which he preferred. She was married, a commoner, an American and a divorcée. He was seeking the society of a woman who, by the very nature of her situation, did not regard him as the most eligible bachelor in the world.

In the society of this American woman Edward, Prince of Wales, later, King Edward VIII, found an oasis in the arid desert of that official England which he esteemed and for which he could make allowances.

Chapter II

MAYFAIR WHISPERS : AMERICA TALKS

It WAS SOME TIME BEFORE MAYFAIR
and the foreign Press began to notice the week-end
parties at Fort Belvedere and to take stock of
the fact that the principals in the story were
beginning to see more and more of each other.
But at length the question arose : Who is Mrs.
Simpson ? The interest of Mayfair soon became
intense.

The story of Mrs. Simpson's career was rapidly
pieced together from the details which gradually
found their way into the pages of the American
Press.

Mrs. Simpson was born in Baltimore, Maryland,
in 1896. She was formerly Miss Bessie Wallis

Warfield, daughter of Teakle Wallis Warfield, a relative of Governor Warfield of Maryland. She was an only child, and her father died when she was three.

Her mother was left in rather straitened circumstances, and for some time took paying guests, a fact that led the American newspapers to describe with romantic colour how her daughter "Wally" helped to attend to the boarders. She was, however, only a small child at that time.

At the age of twelve she went to live with a wealthy uncle, Mr. Solomon Davies Warfield, who later became president of the Seaboard Airline Co. She attended some of the best schools in the city, and made her entry into Baltimore "society" at the age of eighteen. Two years later, in 1916, she met, while staying with relations at Pensacola, in Florida, Lieutenant Earl Wingfield Spencer, of Chicago, an instructor at a naval aviation station. They were married and lived at Pensacola for two years, when Lieutenant Spencer was sent to California to establish a naval flying school.

In July, 1927, Mrs. Spencer filed a bill of complaint to show that her husband had deserted her and had contributed nothing to her support since

24

1922. An uncontested divorce was granted on these grounds at Warrenton, Virginia.

On July 28, 1928, she married Mr. Ernest Aldrich Simpson in London. Mr. Simpson was the son of Mr. Ernest L. Simpson, of New York, a leading shipbroker, of the firm of Simpson, Spence and Young, of New York and London. Mr. Simpson, senr., was an Englishman, and his wife an American. As a Harvard undergraduate the son had enlisted, in 1918, in the Coldstream Guards and had received a commission. After the War he returned to Harvard and graduated. He married Dorothea Parsons Dechert, but that marriage was dissolved. There was one child.

Mr. and Mrs. Simpson entertained a great deal in London and entered an Anglo-American Society group in which the Prince of Wales had many friends. Mrs. Simpson soon proved her capacity as hostess. Her small, exclusive dinners and her cocktail parties became famous. It was observed that the Prince of Wales was a frequent visitor. The younger society of Mayfair began to clamour for invitations to these exclusive gatherings.

When it was realized that Mrs. Simpson was a warm friend of the Prince speculation grew apace. After the death of King George, it was apparent that King Edward did not intend to sever his former relations, and speculation assumed the wings of scandal. A constitutional crisis appeared imminent.

And then on Derby Day—May 27, 1936—the names of Mr. and Mrs. Ernest Simpson appeared in the Court Circular—for the first time—as having dined with the King. Mayfair was bewildered and amazed. Westminster was astonished. Many comforted themselves with the reflection that only Col. and Mrs. Lindbergh and Mr. and Mrs. Stanley Baldwin had been guests at St. James's, and that therefore the small indiscretion might be overlooked.

The news escaped the comment of the man-in-the-street, but Mayfair was quick to grasp its implications. It was apparent that Edward VIII was not renouncing his five-year-old friendship. The implications were strengthened on July 10, 1936, when the following announcement appeared in the Court Circular :

"The King gave a dinner party at York House this evening, at which the Duke and Duchess of York were present. The following had the

26

honour of being invited : The Marquess and Marchioness of Willingdon, the Lady Diana Cooper, the Earl and Countess of Stanhope, the Countess of Oxford and Asquith, Major the Hon. Alexander and Mrs. Hardinge, the Rt. Hon. Winston Spencer Churchill, M.P., and Mrs. Spencer Churchill, the Rt. Hon. Sir Samuel Hoare, the Rt. Hon. Sir Philip Sassoon, Bt., M.P., Captain the Rt. Hon. David Margesson, M.P., Sir Edward and Lady Peacock, Lady Colefax, and Mrs. Ernest Simpson."

That was the King's answer. Mrs. Simpson had attended, unescorted by her husband. It was also his answer to the American Press. For while Mayfair had whispered, America had begun to talk. And when the American Press is on such a story it uses its loudest notes.

In face of all this the British Press held its peace. The story of this reticence will be read as a tribute to its patience. Even when the King sailed down the Adriatic in Lady Yule's yacht, *Nahlin*, with Mrs. Ernest Simpson aboard, again unaccompanied by her husband, the Press maintained its silence. Very few pictures crept into the newspapers. None of them were featured.

The romance and the temptation to "splash" it were peculiarly strong for American journalists. Here was a King, the Monarch of an Empire so vast as to be beyond the vision of a Gibbon, and an American girl. It struck the imagination, and the readers of their journals could not get enough of the story. In Vienna and in Budapest the King and the girl were seen dancing together.

"Prince Edward Rumbas With U.S. Girl." Here was a headline which ripped the latest gangster right out of the news. It was a story to titillate a cinema-ridden democracy better than Hollywood could ever do. How often had they danced together? What were the tunes? How was she dressed? And when facts could not supply the answers to the anxious questions of their readers, imagination was called upon and the answers found. By the time Edward, Prince of Wales, had succeeded to the throne of his father, a whole legend had been gathered to link his name with that of Wallis Warfield Spencer Simpson.

No wonder the American visitor to our shores smiled a little contemptuously at the poor Britisher who had yet to know of this great story. Into England poured the star reporters and the sob-sisters of America. Nothing could satisfy the palates of their readers. Italy could reduce Abyssinia to a shambles ; the League of Nations could be flouted by Germany, Italy and Japan ; General Franco could deluge Spain with her own blood ; that was nothing in comparison with the possibility of Mrs. Simpson becoming the Queen of England.

Thus, while the British Press maintained an austere silence, America awoke daily to a fresh sensation. "King Chooses Clothes To Match Mrs. Simpson's", screamed one headline. "Palace Car And Chauffeur At Mrs. Simpson's Disposal", shrieked another. When they got tired of calling her "Mrs. Simpson" they called her "Wallis", Soon she was just plain "Wally", and every American's darling. Then the speculation grew. In some things they forecast correctly ; at times they published deliberate untruths. When they announced in the boldest headlines known to American journalism that the "King Might Quit Throne To Wed Wally" they guessed correctly ; but when they stated that the "Simpson Divorce Excites London" they were wilfully wide of the mark, if by London they meant London, and not

Mayfair. Thus the American Press put the King of England and Mrs. Simpson on the spot—and kept them there.

During this time Cabinet Ministers, Members of Parliament and other English notabilities, according to their later confessions, were being deluged with cuttings from the American Press. Still, however, not a whisper escaped into the British Press. Mayfair, however, was beginning to talk aloud, and at this point the centre of its interest was transferred to Ipswich, where divorce proceedings brought by Mrs. Simpson against her husband were heard by Mr. Justice Hawke on October 27.

Mrs. Simpson complained before the court that Ernest Simpson had been guilty of adultery with a woman named in the depositions. Her case was conducted by Mr. Norman Birkett and was undefended. A decree *nisi* was pronounced.

Chapter III

STANLEY BALDWIN INTERVENES

Newspaper reports in America now began to take a graver turn. Up to this time they had been personal and gossipy. Just before the divorce the Hearst journals blazoned across the continent, from the Atlantic to the Pacific that

> "Within a few days Mrs. Ernest Simpson, of Baltimore, Mass., U.S.A., will obtain her decree in England, and some eight months thereafter she will be married to Edward VIII, King of England."

Mr. William Randolph Hearst was at this time spending a holiday at his castle, St. Donats,

Wales, and had an interview with the King's Assistant Private Secretary, Sir Godfrey Thomas.

Coloured accounts of the twenty-seven minutes' proceedings at Ipswich were spread across almost endless columns.

British newspapers confined the report to a few lines tucked away in obscure columns. Some did not mention it at all. By the beginning of November the American clippings were pouring in to make up in Mayfair for what the British editors had missed. Swiftly now the gossip spread through Fleet Street and Westminster. Members of Parliament, public officials and journalists besieged the bookstalls for foreign journals. Most of the journals were available, but in numbers quite inadequate to the demand. Buyers discovered, moreover, that even if they were fortunate enough to secure copies they did not contain the precious news for which they had been bought. The journals were sold to the public with the offending passages deleted or with the wanted pages missing. This continued for weeks, and perturbed purchasers were quick to cry out against the unofficial censorship. Complaint soon pushed its way into the parliamentary lobbies.

By the middle of November considerable sections in London's political and religious circles were athirst for news. The ban on foreign papers and the long-maintained silence of the British Press were discussed in private party meetings. The matter was brought to a head in the House of Commons on November 17 when, as Hansard reports :

Mr. Adamson asked the President of the Board of Trade "whether there is any special scrutiny of books and printed literature imported from other countries, and whether he can state the quantities and value, respectively, of scientific, historical, and artistic books, in addition to novels, which were imported from the United States of America during the last full year available."

Mr. Runciman : "It is not clear what exactly the hon. member has in mind. If he will give particulars either to me or my right honourable friend, the Financial Secretary to the Treasury, inquiries will be made, and he will be informed of the result. As regards the second part of the question, I regret that the information asked for is not available, as books of the kinds mentioned are not separately distinguished in the official records."

Mr. Adamson : "Is the right hon. gentleman

33

aware that a considerable quantity of such literature is coming into this country, and that it is
mentioned in the statistical returns of his own
Department ; and can he give any information
as to the types of literature that does come in ?"

Mr. Runciman : "I am afraid that I cannot go
further than the answer which I have already
given to the House."

Miss Wilkinson : "Can the right honourable
gentleman say why, in the case of two American
magazines of high repute imported into this
country during the last few weeks, at least two,
and sometimes three, pages have been torn out ;
and what is this thing the British public are not
allowed to see ?"

Mr. Runciman : "My department has nothing
to do with that."

Mr. Rathbone : "May I ask my right honourable
friend whether the magazines referred to can
seriously be considered as being of high repute ?"

This brief interrogation indicated the manner in
which the House was lining up on the unofficial
censorship, but it did nothing to allay the ban
exercised by the wholesalers. The scrutiny of
incoming journals was continued.

Seven days prior to the divorce action—on
October 20—Mr. Baldwin sought and secured his

first audience of the King concerning "the difficult situation which might arise" from His Majesty's association with Mrs. Simpson. The Premier has told of this highly important meeting. It is plain that the Cabinet was growing uneasy over the spread of criticism in America.

Mr. Baldwin said subsequently in Parliament that he did not press the King for any kind of an answer to his suggestions. Nor did he discuss the matter again until November 16, on the eve of the King's departure for a three-days' tour of the distressed areas in South Wales. On this occasion it was the King who sent for Mr. Baldwin.

In his now world-famous speech Mr. Baldwin has recounted that fateful meeting. For some days he had been perturbed by the news of the granting of a decree *nisi*. Now he heard at Buckingham Palace of the King's intentions.

Mr. Baldwin told His Majesty that he did not think that a particular marriage was one that would receive the approbation of the country, for the marriage which the King had in mind involved the question of the lady becoming Queen of England.

This was, indeed, a fateful moment in the history of the country. The King, in answer to his Prime Minister's advice, said : "I am going to marry Mrs. Simpson and I am prepared to go."

With that portentous sentence Mr. Baldwin went back to Downing Street, leaving the King to make his preparations for his visit to South Wales.

This tour was generally regarded as the most important ever undertaken by a British Monarch. In the grim misery of these derelict valleys he was greeted on all sides by the populace as a harbinger of hope, a promise of better times. All the newspapers emphasized the impression he made on the people and the no less profound impression their conditions made on him.

In the course of this tour—during which he sent for Mr. Malcolm Stewart, Commissioner for the Special Areas, who had recently resigned after submitting to the Cabinet an outspoken report—he visited the "dead town" of Dowlais, in Glamorganshire, where he said "something ought to be done to find these people employment".

Before he left South Wales he had comforted tens of thousands of unemployed people by the further statement that "something will be done".

The Press comment on the tour was typified by the *News-Chronicle* leader :

"The King is above and outside politics. What he has done is in the sole interest of truth and public service. . . . The man in the street feels that Whitehall stands condemned."

The Times countered with a reprimand :

"The King's Ministers are His Majesty's advisers, and to contrast his personal and representative concern for the well-being of a section of the people with the administrative slips of his advisers is a constitutionally dangerous proceeding and would threaten, if continued, to entangle the Throne in politics."

The *Daily Mail*, approving that "something will be done", contrasted the King's energy with what it alleged to be the Government's inertia.

On November 20 the King was back again in London. Events then began to move rapidly. On Wednesday, November 25, he sent for Mr. Baldwin and asked him whether he had considered the alternative of Mrs. Simpson becoming his wife but not his Consort. Mr. Baldwin replied that he had not considered it formally but, if the King wished it, he would submit the proposal to the Cabinet and communicate with the Prime Ministers of the Dominion Governments. The King said that he did so wish.

Mr. Baldwin placed the matter before his colleagues at a hurriedly convened Cabinet Meeting on Friday, November 27. This meeting was placarded by the evening newspapers as being concerned with Spain, but certain of the dailies the next morning hinted at the discussion being actually concerned with a difference between the King and his Ministers.

This same day the *Church Times*, a weekly, made some critical observations on the King in a leading article.

The week-end passed without remark. During the past few days Parliament had been giving further attention to the Special Areas in which the public had become considerably interested as a result of the Royal tour, and was also contemplating the passage of a Bill to prevent the transport of arms to Spain by British ships.

What public interest had already been aroused —which was little beyond the limited circles in London—was for a day forgotten by the outbreak of fire which on Monday, November 30, destroyed the Crystal Palace.

UNIVERSITY OF WINNIPEG
LIBRARY
515 Portage Avenue
Winnipeg, Manitoba R3B 2E9

Chapter IV

BISHOP BLUNT PROTESTS

THE NEXT DAY—TUESDAY, DECEMBER 1,
—the news so many had been awaiting began to
break. The Bishop of Bradford, Dr. Alfred Walter
Frank Blunt, addressing his Diocesan Conference
at Bradford, among other things, said :

"The benefit of the King's Coronation depends,
under God, upon two elements—first on the faith,
prayer, and self-dedication of the King himself—
and on that it would be improper for me to say
anything except commend him, and ask you to
commend him, to God's grace, which he will so
abundantly need, as we all need it—for the King
is a man like ourselves—if he is to do his duty
faithfully. We hope that he is aware of his need.
Some of us wish that he gave more positive signs
of his awareness.

39

"But let me emphasize one point which, I think, is very material for a proper understanding of the intention of the service. It is this, that on this occasion, the King holds an avowedly representative position. His personal views and opinions are his own, and as an individual he has the right of us all to be the keeper of his own private conscience. But in his public capacity at his Coronation he stands for the English people's idea of kingship. It has for long centuries been, and I hope, still is, an essential part of that idea that the King needs the grace of God for his office. In the Coronation ceremony the nation definitely acknowledges that need. Whatever it may mean, much or little, to the individual who is crowned, to the people as a whole it means their dedication of the English Monarchy to the care of God, in whose rule and governance are the hearts of kings.

"Thus, in the second place, not only as important, but far more important, than the King's personal feelings are to his Coronation, are the feelings with which we—the people of England—view it. Our part in the ceremony is to fill it with reality, by the sincerity of our belief in the power of God to overrule for good our national history, and by the sincerity with which we commend King and Nation to His providence."

The report was immediately flashed by the Press Association at 4.30 p.m. to all the newspaper offices. The Association drew special attention to the critical passages. All the newspapers reported the speech—which was widely believed to have been inspired—but it was left to certain provincial papers to feature the story and to pass comment. These particular newspapers felt that the reproof administered by Dr. Blunt need not be condemned because it had been levelled at a king, and welcomed the direct raising of the personal aspect of the situation in which the King now found himself.

The chorus from the provinces rather staggered both the Cabinet and Fleet Street. The London journals waited and watched developments. They appreciated the fact that a Cabinet meeting which had lasted from 11 a.m. to 1.20 p.m. on Friday, November 27, was one having far-reaching importance. It now became known that Mr. Baldwin had seen the King that same evening, and the whispers grew. On December 2 the *Manchester Guardian* was speaking openly of a "constitutional issue". It said :

". . . there is reason to think that the hastily summoned Cabinet meeting of Friday was concerned not with the troubled state of Europe, but with a domestic problem that involves an important constitutional issue, since it bears on the relation of the King to his Ministers, and his readiness to be guided, in all matters which may affect the welfare of the British Commonwealth by the advice which the Prime Minister sees fit to offer."

Very little appeared in the London evening newspapers, except extracts from the provincial comments, and news that Coronation insurance rates were rising.

But there was great perturbation in the offices of the London dailies as they prepared on this Wednesday night their Thursday editions. They had been reticent for nearly six months. Now the decision had to be finally and hurriedly taken.

Indicative of the confusion were the headlines, spread over the same story and full across the page, of two editions of the *Daily Mirror*. First edition read : "Baldwin's Hour-and-a-Half Talk With The King : Grave Issue". The second : "The King Wants To Marry Mrs. Simpson : Cabinet Advises 'No'."

At last the problems and principals had gained

the public light. Reason for the rift in the long shroud of silence was admitted by *The Times* : "It is a simple fact that the American campaign of publicity, so long and so wisely ignored in this country, has now reached a point at which it goes far beyond that side of His Majesty's life which may justly be held to be private."

Yet even now *The Times* did not follow its argument to its logical conclusion. In its news columns it simply mentioned that Mr. Baldwin had seen the King ; its leader discussed the problem without mentioning Mrs. Simpson by name.

Conjecture and rumour were now being confirmed by fact. Sir John Simon, acting in place of Lord Hailsham, the Lord Chancellor, who had been ill for some time, was having frequent discussions with the Premier. A long meeting on Thursday evening of the senior members of the Government testified to the supposition that important developments were to be expected.

Wednesday, December 2, had seen that delicate barometer, the Stock Exchange, react to the situation. Buying prices in the Consols Market were from one to two points below the previous day's quotations. Comparable changes were also

43

shown in the industrials and miscellaneous markets. The absence of any great offering of sterling from abroad indicated that the decline was of domestic origin.

Thursday, December 3, found the story in full flood. This may be regarded as the day on which the crisis—as it came to be called—began. All the London journals featured the news and carried long leading articles. The matter which had hitherto excited profound interest in select circles now became a matter of common concern.

The Bishop of Bradford had, meanwhile, issued a statement in which he said : "I studiously took care to say nothing with regard to his private life, because I know nothing about it."

Amid the developing excitement the newspapers began to take sides. There was general relief that the facts were now coming into the open, but a large section of the Press was still inclined to criticize Bishop Blunt for what it alleged was interference in the King's private affairs.

The *News-Chronicle*, representing Liberal opinion, began to seek a way out. It proposed that the King should marry Mrs. Simpson as the Duke of Cornwall. This view it continued to advocate

44

until it became acquainted with the obstacles.

While journals like *The Daily Telegraph* were expressing a hope that the King would renounce Mrs. Simpson, the *Daily Herald*, on the assumption that the Cabinet had advised against the marriage, expressed itself as fully in agreement with Government. This view, though somewhat vague, was shared by the other national journals. Implicitly, if not explicitly, there was remarkable unanimity in the opinion that the proposed marriage should not take place.

On Thursday morning Members of Parliament noticed that Col. Josiah Wedgwood had placed on the order paper the following motion :

"In the opinion of this House, the oath of allegiance which they have already taken to King Edward VIII is unaffected by any form of Coronation ceremony, or by the presence thereat, or absence therefrom, of any dignitary or personage whatsoever ; nor will they substitute any other for the King of England."

Colonel Wedgwood's motion brought to the surface rumours which had been simmering in the lobbies since the middle of October when American newspapers had published sensational stories to the effect that the Archbishop of Canterbury had declined to dine with the King in company with Mrs. Simpson and had intimated his intention to refuse to participate in the Coronation ceremony unless the King severed his association with her.

That afternoon when Mr. Baldwin entered the House of Commons to answer a prearranged question by Mr. C. Attlee, the leader of the Labour Opposition, he was greeted with a loud roar of cheering.

Mr. Attlee : "May I ask the Prime Minister the following question, of which I have given him private notice—namely, whether any constitutional difficulties have arisen, and whether he has a statement to make ?"

Mr. Baldwin : "I have no statement to make to-day, but while there does not at present exist any constitutional difficulty, the situation is of such a nature as to make it inexpedient that I should be questioned about it at this stage."

Mr. Attlee : "May I ask the right hon. gentleman whether, in view of the anxiety that these reports are causing in the minds of many people, he can assure the House that he will make a statement at the earliest possible time that a statement can be made ?"

Mr. Baldwin : "I can assure the right hon. gentleman that all that he says I have very much in mind."

Mr. Churchill : "Will my right hon. friend give us an assurance that no irrevocable step will be taken before a formal statement is made to Parliament ?"

Mr. Baldwin : "I have nothing to add to the statement I have made at this present moment. I will consider and examine the question that my right hon. friend has asked."

This closed a rather tense episode. Later, members began to gather themselves together, for it was obvious that history was in a state of suspense. The decision of the King was now the vital factor, and slowly over the Houses of Parliament there came the first hint of abdication. Parliamentary observers were quick to note that the Constitution and the Monarchy could again be made a living issue, and it was evident that within the precincts of Westminster there was a spirit manifesting itself which was transcending party warfare.

This grave hint seeped into the Press, and that evening the story was in full flood. As it hurried through the land men and women became anxious. Which way would the King decide—for the Empire and without the lady, or for a union with Mrs. Simpson and abdication of his throne ?

That evening the Prime Minister paid his third visit to the Palace that week. It was obvious that more than ordinary things were afoot, for when Mr. Baldwin withdrew at 10.40 p.m., the King left Buckingham Palace and went to Marlborough House where he saw Queen Mary and the Duke and Duchess of York. During the day he had seen his brothers, the Duke of Gloucester and the Duke of Kent. After leaving his mother he returned to Buckingham Palace and later left for Fort Belvedere.

On arrival at Fort Belvedere the King had a late consultation with Major Ulick Alexander, the Keeper of the Privy Purse, Colonel the Hon. Piers Legh, his Equerry, and Sir Godfrey Thomas, his Assistant Private Secretary. He also took farewell of Mrs. Simpson, whose car later left the Fort and proceeded towards London. This was evidently a successful ruse, for it was not until the next day that journalists learned that she had crossed to

France *via* Newhaven-Dieppe, proceeded to Rouen, and had rested at the Hotel de la Poste.

During that evening consultations between members of the Government and the Dominions High Commissioners were taking place. Reports from Dominion Premiers were also reaching London.

Mr. Mackenzie King, Canadian Prime Minister, stated : "I do not intend to be drawn into any discussion on this all-important subject by replying to what are unwarrantable rumours." But it was obvious that Canada might easily be offended, for it contains a large proportion of people to whom divorce is abhorrent.

The Australian Federal Cabinet viewed the situation with perturbation, but Mr. Lyons refused to make any statement. His Parliament, it was stated, had been summoned for Saturday, December 5.

Nervousness had manifested itself on the Johannesburg Stock Exchange, and the *Cape Argus* hoped that "uneasiness and anxiety would still be happily resolved".

Chapter V

PARLIAMENT TAKES ITS STAND

FRIDAY, DECEMBER 4, HAS BEEN designated the turning point of the crisis. There was deep concern in the Dominions. The *Melbourne Argus* summarized the feelings of British subjects beyond the seas. "The King", it said, "is a man among men, a soldier and a comrade. It is impossible, however, to dissociate personal properties from kingly responsibilities. The Throne is sanctified by the tradition that is in Britain's fibre. Its march must be continuous on a high level of conduct ever illumined with the burnished light of sacrifice". In London excitement rose as the day moved on to the hour when Mr. Baldwin was expected to make his statement.

Meanwhile, on the Friday evening, December 4, the Archbishop of Canterbury issued a statement:

"At this moment of deep anxiety and bewilderment in the public mind I venture to express two earnest hopes.

"The first is that, during this critical week-end, and especially on Sunday, those who have a duty to speak to the people from the pulpit or otherwise will refrain from speaking directly on the matters which have arisen affecting the King himself and his subjects.

"Words spoken with imperfect knowledge of an extremely difficult situation can give no helpful guidance, and may only mislead or confuse public thought and feeling. Silence is fitting until the ultimate decisions are made known.

"Secondly, I hope, and indeed I take it for granted, that on Sunday prayers will be offered in all our churches, as surely they must be continually offered in the hearts of all Christian people, that God may in these momentous hours overrule the decisions of the King and of his Government for the lasting good of the Realm and Empire."

This same Friday, the newspapers were spreading the news under gigantic headlines. They came out with pages of pictures, life-stories of the King and of Mrs. Simpson, chronological records of the crisis. Editions of enlarged papers were printed in enormous numbers.

The most significant event of this exciting day in Fleet Street was a divergence of Lord Beaverbrook's and Lord Rothermere's papers from the previous unanimous support accorded to the Cabinet : the *Daily Express*, the *Daily Mail*, the *Evening Standard* and the *Evening News* began to criticize Mr. Baldwin and strongly resented any solution that might mean the loss of King Edward.

It was soon clear that the British Government had the backing of all the Dominion Governments, and slowly there came the conviction that there was no possibility of a compromise being effected.

The world was now watching Mrs. Simpson's dash across France to Cannes, pursued by scores of journalists and Press photographers. Hounded by these people, unable to make even a rational use of hotels on the way, at times forced to eat her meals in her car with blinds drawn, often returning on her tracks in order to escape the attentions of her pursuers, she finally arrived at the Villa Lou

Viei, the home of Mr. and Mrs. Herman Rogers, American friends.

At Vienne Mrs. Simpson said to Press representatives : "The King alone is judge. I have nothing to say except that I want to be left quiet."

With Mrs. Simpson travelled a Lord-in-Waiting to the King—Lord Brownlow.

Saturday—December 5—proved a busy day for the Premier. After a forty-five minute meeting of the Cabinet, Mr. Baldwin had three consultations with Sir John Simon which lasted in all nearly seven hours. That evening he again motored out to Fort Belvedere and had an audience of an hour and a quarter with the King. This was the fifth audience of the week. On his return to Downing Street it was announced that a Cabinet Meeting was called for Sunday evening.

Saturday was not to pass without a further intervention by Mr. Churchill, who issued the following statement to the Press :

"I plead for time and patience. The nation must realize the character of the constitutional issue. There is no question of any conflict between the King and Parliament. Parliament has not been consulted in any way, nor allowed to express any opinion.

"The question is whether the King is to abdicate upon the advice of the Ministry of the day. No such advice has ever before been tendered to a Sovereign in Parliamentary times.

"This is not a case where differences have arisen between the Sovereign and his Ministers on any particular measure. These could certainly be resolved by normal processes of Parliament or dissolution.

"In this case we are in presence of a wish expressed by the Sovereign to perform an act which in no circumstances can be accomplished for nearly five months, and may conceivably, for various reasons, never be accomplished at all.

"That, on such a hypothetical and supposititious basis the supreme sacrifice of abdication and potential exile of the Sovereign should be demanded, finds no support whatever in the British constitution. No Ministry has the authority to advise the abdication of the Sovereign. Only the most serious Parliamentary processes could even raise the issue in a decisive form.

"The Cabinet has no right to prejudge such a question without having previously ascertained at the very least the will of Parliament. This could, perhaps, be obtained by messages from the Sovereign to Parliament, and by addresses of both Houses after due consideration of these messages.

"For the Sovereign to abdicate incontinently

in the present circumstances would inflict an injury upon the constitutional position of the monarchy which is measureless and cannot fail to be grievous to the institution itself, irrespective of the existing occupant of the Throne.

"Parliament would also fail entirely in its duty if it allowed such an event to occur as the signing of an abdication in response to the advice of Ministers without taking all precautions to make sure that these same processes may not be repeated with equal uncanny facility at no distant date in unforeseen circumstances. Clearly time is needed for searching constitutional debate.

"The next question is—What has the King done ? If it be true, as is alleged, that the King has proposed to his Ministers legislation which they are not prepared to introduce, the answer of Ministers should be not to call for abdication, but to refuse to act upon the King's request, which thereupon becomes inoperative.

"If the King refuses to take the advice of his Ministers they are, of course, free to resign. They have no right whatever to put pressure upon him to accept their advice by soliciting beforehand assurances from the Leader of the Opposition that he will not form an alternative Administration in the event of their resignation, and thus confronting the King with an ultimatum. Again, there is cause for time and patience.

"Why cannot time be granted ? The fact that it is beyond the King's power to accomplish the purpose which Ministers oppose until the end of April surely strips the matter of constitutional urgency.

"There may be some inconvenience, but that inconvenience stands on a different plane altogether from the grave constitutional issues I have set forth.

"National and Imperial considerations alike require that before such a dread step as a demand for abdication is taken, not only should the constitutional position be newly defined by Parliament, but that every method should be exhausted which gives the hope of a happier solution.

"Lastly, but surely not least, there is the human and personal aspect.

"The King has been for many weeks under the greatest strain, moral and mental, that can fall upon a man. Not only has he been inevitably subjected to the extreme stress of his public duty, but also to the agony of his own personal feelings.

"Surely, if he asks for time to consider the advice of his Ministers, now that at length matters have been brought to this dire culmination, he should not be denied.

"Howsoever this matter may turn, it is pregnant with calamity and inseparable from inconvenience. But all the evil aspects will be aggravated beyond measure if the utmost chivalry and compassion is not shown, both by Ministers and by the British nation, towards a gifted and beloved King torn between private and public obligations of love and duty.

"The Churches stand for charity. They believe in the efficacy of prayer. Surely their influence must not oppose a period of reflection. I plead, I pray, that time and tolerance will not be denied.

"The King has no means of personal access to his Parliament or his people. Between him and them stand in their office the Ministers of the Crown. If they thought it their duty to engage all their power and influence against him, still he must remain silent.

"All the more must they be careful not to be the judge in their own case, and to show a loyal and Christian patience even at some political embarrassment to themselves.

"If an abdication were to be hastily extorted the outrage so committed would cast its shadow forward across many chapters of the history of the British Empire."

Sunday morning came with the Sunday newspapers doing their best to make up in one week-end for all the advantage their American contemporaries had gained on them in months.

Special editions were published in the evening

from which a surprised public learned that a specially summoned meeting of senior Ministers had taken place in the morning. Mr. Baldwin left this meeting for a consultation with Queen Mary, which lasted half an hour, and returned to his colleagues. It was noticed that Sir Donald Somervell, the Attorney-General, was at this meeting. Sir Donald was not a member of the Cabinet. As he had dined with Mr. Baldwin the previous evening, significance was attached to the Attorney-General's presence.

Before this meeting began Mr. W. T. Monckton, K.C., Attorney-General to the Duchy of Cornwall, had been in consultation with the Premier. Mr. Monckton had been constantly travelling between Downing Street and Fort Belvedere during the past few days and had held long audiences of the King and interviews with Mr. Baldwin.

That afternoon the Archbishop of Canterbury paid a visit to No. 10. As he arrived at the door Sir Archibald Sinclair, the Liberal leader, left. It was at this moment that a demonstration occurred. A man shouting "We want the King—and his wife !" was led out of the famous street after he had scattered a handful of papers. Great crowds were gathering in Whitehall, and the police had some difficulty in controlling them.

The Cabinet Meeting took place at 5.30 p.m. and lasted until after 7 p.m. Half an hour before it ended Mr. Monckton again entered No. 10, having arrived from Fort Belvedere in one of the King's cars.

The King had remained at Fort Belvedere over the week-end. It was known that he was beginning to feel the strain. All afternoon motorists were pulling up outside the gates of the Fort, and the cry of "God Save the King !" was heard.

Lord Craigavon, Prime Minister of Northern Ireland, had paid a visit to the Prime Minister on the Saturday evening, and he added to the week-end comment by telling the reporters : "I have nothing to say ; but 'Trust Baldwin'."

On Sunday evening a great crowd collected outside Buckingham Palace, but there was no disorder nor hostile demonstration.

The morning papers on Monday, December 7, were beginning to feel depressed. Some, notably the *Daily Mirror*, had over the week-end swung round against the Cabinet, talked vaguely in terms of a "King's Party". It was suggested that many false impressions had gathered about the relations between His Majesty and the Prime Minister. Chief among these was the suggestion that Mr. Baldwin had been tendering advice which amounted almost to an ultimatum involving either the abdication of the King or the resignation of the Government. It was obvious that such a development was implicit in the situation, but, despite Mr. Churchill's criticism that the Cabinet had behaved unreasonably, an important section of the Press, which had all along supported Mr. Baldwin, insisted that the advice given to the King was only that which he had sought. Nor, they maintained, was he being hastened to a decision.

The simple fact was that the Government was not prepared to legislate to procure morganatic marriage.

This appeared to induce many leading newspapers to counsel delay. This attitude, symptomatic of the rising excitement, was expressed when the House of Commons met in the afternoon. In a crowded Chamber—into which the Prime Minister had entered amid cheers—Colonel Josiah Wedgwood rose to ask if he would be given an early opportunity to discuss the motion standing in his name.

Mr. Baldwin answered curtly, "No, sir."

"Arising out of that answer," cried Colonel Wedgwood, "may I ask the right honourable gentleman whether he can at least give us an assurance that the fatal and final step of abdication or acceptance of abdication—" His words were lost in a roar of protest.

Thus Parliament heard for the first time the dreaded word "abdication".

The noise allayed, Mr. Attlee rose in his place and quietly put this question :

"May I ask the Prime Minister whether he has anything to add to the statement which he made on Friday?"

Mr. Baldwin : "Yes, sir. I am glad to have the occasion of making a further statement on the position.

"In considering the whole matter it has always been, and remains, the earnest desire of the Government to afford to His Majesty the fullest opportunity of weighing a decision which involves so directly his own future happiness and the interests of all his subjects.

"At the same time they cannot but be aware that any considerable prolongation of the present state of suspense and uncertainty would involve risk of the gravest injury to national and imperial

E   63

interests, and indeed no one is more insistent upon this aspect of the situation than His Majesty.

"In view of certain statements which have been made about the relations between the Government and the King, I should add that, with the exception of the question of morganatic marriage, no advice has been tendered by the Government to His Majesty, with whom all my conversations have been strictly personal and informal.

"These matters were not raised first by the Government, but by His Majesty himself, in conversation with me some weeks ago, when he first informed me of his intention to marry Mrs. Simpson whenever she should be free.

"The subject has therefore been for some time in the King's mind, and as soon as His Majesty has arrived at a conclusion as to the course he desires to take, he will no doubt communicate it to his Governments in this country and the Dominions.

"It will then be for those Governments to decide what advice, if any, they would feel it their duty to tender to him in the light of his conclusion.

"I cannot conclude this statement without expressing—what the whole House feels—our deep and respectful sympathy with His Majesty at this time."

Mr. Baldwin resumed his seat amid a storm of cheers and Mr. Attlee rose and said :

"Everyone will agree with the sympathy expressed by the Prime Minister in the last words of his statement. I am assuming from his statement that his Majesty has not yet come to a decision on the advice tendered to him on a morganatic marriage, and if this is so it is difficult to press the Prime Minister for a further explanation at the present time.

"But I would like to ask him to bear in mind, as I am sure he does, that the House and the country is deeply anxious to receive the fullest information as soon as possible, as without that it is not possible to have any proper discussion on these issues."

The Premier replied :

"I am obliged to the right hon. gentleman for the point he has put, and I am grateful to him. I agree with every word of what he says. I shall be only too glad at a suitable moment to give the House any information I am able to, and, while I am always willing to answer supplementary questions, I think the whole House will agree with me that at this moment, when the situation is so grave and anxious and while the King is considering these matters and has not yet made up his mind, I should feel great difficulty in offering information and answering supplementary questions, especially when considering the answers I shall have to give will have to be improvized."

At the first opportunity Mr. Churchill rose to put his supplementary question in which he requested an assurance that no irrevocable steps would be taken. He was met with a loud roar of "Order !" "Sit down !" and "Shut up !"

He was patently taken aback and remained standing, but further discussion was impossible and he resumed his seat, after a mild rebuke from the Speaker.

After Mr. George Lambert had assured Mr. Baldwin that "there is in this House deep personal sympathy with him", Mr. Baldwin rose, and looking directly at Mr. Churchill, said : "I do not know yet, and cannot know yet, what the King may decide or how he may decide to act. It is quite impossible for me to enter into hypothetical questions."

When Mr. Baldwin sat down, Mr. Gallagher rose in his place and put a supplementary question which caused a great deal of comment later. He said : "I would like to ask the Prime Minister if it is not the case that this crisis expresses a deeper crisis in the economic system ?"

It was obvious to a packed gallery that Mr. Baldwin carried all but a small fraction of the House with him.

A similar statement was communicated to a well-filled House of Lords by Lord Halifax on the same afternoon.

Meanwhile the King was awaiting the issue at Fort Belvedere. Mr. Monckton, K.C., who had spent the night there, left shortly after 9.30 a.m. in a Royal car for Buckingham Palace where, with Sir Edward Peacock, Receiver-General of the Duchy of Lancaster, he had a conference with officials of the King's household. Later Mr. Monckton had a consultation with Mr. Baldwin which lasted over two hours.

After his departure from the House of Commons about nine o'clock, Mr. Baldwin went back to No. 10 Downing Street, where he received two further visitors who arrived in a Palace car. It was assumed that one of these was the King's secretary.

That night the Duke of York dined with the

King at Fort Belvedere and from Cannes came the news that Lord Brownlow had read a statement by Mrs. Simpson to a group of journalists.

"Mrs. Simpson," the statement announced, "throughout the last few weeks has invariably wished to avoid any action or proposal which would hurt or damage His Majesty or the Throne.

"To-day her attitude is unchanged, and she is willing, if such action would solve the problem, to withdraw forthwith from a situation that has been rendered unhappy and untenable."*

The statement by Mrs. Simpson was held to be a way out of the deadlock, and the newspapers seized upon it with avidity. But they reckoned without the King.

---

* Some doubt was cast on this report on December 9th, when Lord Brownlow said to the *Evening Standard* : "Mrs. Simpson has signed no document whatever." This denial may have referred to rumours that Mrs. Simpson had been in consultation with her solicitor, Mr. Theodore Goddard (who had flown to Cannes), regarding the disposal of certain property. If it was intended to refer to the report it looked dangerously like a quibble, for the Press had merely said that Lord Brownlow had read a statement on behalf of Mrs. Simpson. It mattered little whether or not she had signed it.

Chapter VI

THE KING MAKES HIS CHOICE

THE EVENTS OF MONDAY, COMMUNI-
cated to the country by the Press in the evening
and on the following morning, calmed the fears of
many who had protested that the personal affairs
of the King might be dragged into the political
arena. Mr. Baldwin's calm and concise statement
was accepted with general relief, and though it
could not, by the nature of the case, throw much
light on the King's own intentions it nevertheless
assured the country that the Cabinet was guilty of
nothing precipitate and that His Majesty was being
accorded full opportunity to arrive at a considered
decision. Mrs. Simpson's gesture too, a message of
self-abnegation, did much to ease the tension. The

King appeared to the multitude as a man in charge of his own destiny.

The anti-Government section of the Press was now somewhat confused, and gradually veered round again to complete, if still slightly critical, support of the Government. From this point the newspapers may be said to have recovered their original unanimity. The change marked the third and last of three stages. First they were confused but on the whole favourable to the Cabinet's attitude. Then came the breach where a section—chiefly the "popular" dailies and evenings—in their sympathy for the King became vigorously hostile to the Government. Finally the general tone, though not a whit less sympathetic to His Majesty personally, became almost unanimously pro-Government.

So far as the Labour Opposition was concerned —and it might be taken that Mr. Attlee spoke for the entire Opposition—the sooner the matter was settled the better. Mr. Churchill had ceased to oppose, and whatever there had been of a "King's Party" had now collapsed.

It became known during the day that Mr. Churchill had refused to broadcast to America over the Columbia Broadcasting System, and also that Lord Beaverbrook and Lord Rothermere had declined to contribute to the daily talks to U.S.A., in which Professor Laski, a recognized authority on the Constitution, and Lord Ponsonby had already participated.

Nevertheless, despite these consoling factors, Tuesday, December 8, was a day of great suspense. The very fact that the issues had been clarified and the principals thrown into relief opened up the possibility of a real constitutional crisis. In the popular mind the question arose as to whether the King might decline to confine his choice to the marriage or the crown and insist that he was constitutionally entitled—since there was no definite precedent against him—to select his own wife and retain his crown.

In London, especially, since it was, as it were, the seat of the crisis, rumour was rife. Much of the unsavoury detail which had appeared in the American papers had by now percolated into the British Press—suggestions of acrimonious differences between the King and the Church, the King and his Ministers and officials on all kind of questions, public and private, most of them far removed from either horn of the present dilemma. This was the result of the Government's tardiness in revealing the facts and the long continued reticence on the part of the Press.

In official circles nothing of importance occurred during the morning. Sir John Simon spent two hours with Mr. Baldwin, and Sir Samuel Hoare was present at most of this discussion. Mr. Baldwin lunched with Lord Halifax, and did not put in an appearance in the House of Commons that day.

When Mr. Attlee rose in the afternoon to put his daily question—"Has the Prime Minister anything to add to the statement of yesterday?"—Sir John Simon replied that he had nothing further to say.

The Parliamentary lobbies seethed with members and the main topic was the crisis. In official circles it was freely predicted that the King would abdicate. There was to be a Cabinet Meeting on Wednesday morning (December 9), and it was also believed that Mr. Baldwin would proceed from that meeting to the House with the King's decision in his pocket.

The Parliamentary Labour Party met on Tuesday to consider the situation, and although no vote was taken the great majority of the Party showed that they approved the Government's action.

The rumour, which had become current as the days had passed, that Mr. Attlee had been approached and had given an undertaking not to form a Government in the event of Mr. Baldwin resigning, was now thoroughly dispelled. On the Opposition benches it was generally accepted that Mr. Baldwin's handling of the situation had been masterly, and so it would continue.

A whiff of excitement blew across the newspapers in the evening when it became known that a specially chartered Imperial Airways liner had left Croydon for Cannes at 9.30 that morning, carrying three passengers—Mr. Theodore Goddard, Mrs. Simpson's solicitor, his clerk, Mr. Sidney Barron, and Dr. W. Kirkwood.

Certain facts connected with the flight brought forth the wildest speculations. Not only was the aeroplane specially chartered, but it was flown in the teeth of bad flying weather. Dr. Kirkwood was a gynæcologist. Rumour ran wild until it was pointed out that Dr. Kirkwood was also Mr. Goddard's doctor and was accompanying him because Mr. Goddard thought that he might have need of his professional services on this, his first flight. It was later learned that Mr. Goddard had gone to Cannes to discuss the disposal of certain of Mrs. Simpson's property, and that Dr. Kirkwood never approached the villa.

Attention was soon riveted upon Mr. Baldwin, for in the evening he set out with Mr. Monckton, K.C., for his sixth audience of the King and arrived at Fort Belvedere at 5.15 p.m. It was not until after 10 p.m. that he left. During his stay he dined with the King, the Duke of York and the Duke of Kent. The Duke of Kent had been with the King from before midday.

At Downing Street, Sir John Simon had been impatiently awaiting the return of his chief. It was eleven o'clock before Mr. Baldwin reached his home. Sir John Simon stayed with him almost an hour.

That same evening the King's Private Secretary, Major Alexander Hardinge, drove over from Buckingham Palace to Lambeth Palace to see the Primate, Dr. Cosmo Lang.

Simultaneously, news was arriving from the Dominions. Mr. Lyons, Australian Premier, announced that his reassembled Parliament, at Canberra, would adjourn from day to day while awaiting the solution of the crisis. At the same time it was intimated by Australian constitutional authorities like Sir Robert Garran, that if the British Government resigned on this question the Governments in the Dominions must also resign.

Mr. H. Savage, the Prime Minister of New Zealand, requested Mr. A. Hamilton, the Leader of the Opposition, to proceed to Wellington, "since the need for his presence there might arise".

The South African Union Government did not propose to meet earlier than the opening date of the next session, January 8, but it announced that its concurrence in the decisions of the British Government would be automatic.

Towards the close of the day business on the Stock Exchange was again depressed, and reflected a pessimistic view of the constitutional situation.

The suspense of Tuesday was carried into Wednesday (December 9) and became intensified when it was realized that the decision of Edward VIII could not be delayed many hours longer. The Press was beginning to clamour for finality. The Dominions were showing signs of impatience. The eyes of the country were firmly riveted on the King and Mr. Baldwin. It was known that a Cabinet meeting was to take place in the morning, and when it became known that a further meeting was to be called for the evening, the Press began to speak of actual abdication.

Events now followed one another in rapid succession.

9 a.m.—Sir Godfrey Thomas and Mr. Monckton, K.C., left Fort Belvedere by car.

10 a.m.—Sir John Simon arrived at Downing Street for a conversation with the Premier prior to the Cabinet Meeting. Mr. Monckton was present at this talk.

11 a.m.—The Cabinet met and was told of the King's decision.

11.12 a.m.—Mr. Monckton and Sir Edward Peacock, Receiver-General to the Duchy of Cornwall, left No. 10 and went to Buckingham Palace where they had a short consultation with members of the King's staff.

12 noon—Mr. Monckton, K.C., and Sir Edward Peacock returned to Downing Street.

1.15 p.m.—The Cabinet Meeting ended.

1.52 p.m.—Sir Edward Peacock and Mr. Monckton, K.C., left Downing Street together in a Royal car.

2.20 p.m.—Sir John Simon and Mr. Malcolm MacDonald, the Dominions Secretary, left No. 10 and walked across to the Dominions Office. Sir John Simon left Mr. MacDonald there and drove away.

Meanwhile the Royal Family was assembling at the Royal Lodge in Windsor Great Park, the home of the Duke and Duchess of York. Shortly after lunch Queen Mary, accompanied by the Princess Royal and the Earl of Athlone, Queen Mary's brother, left Marlborough House by car for the Royal Lodge. They arrived at 2.15. Immediately afterwards the Duke of York and the Duke of Gloucester arrived, followed a few minutes later by the Duke of Kent. The King, who had not left Fort Belvedere for six days, slipped out of the grounds of the Fort into the grounds of Lord Derby's adjacent estate, and proceeded from there by car to join his family. He arrived at the Royal Lodge shortly before four.

All the members of the Royal Family knew of the King's decision, and for Queen Mary it must have been a distressing experience.

While the Royal Family was meeting in such

trying circumstances, Parliament was waiting to hear if Mr. Baldwin had anything to add to the reply he had given to Mr. Attlee on Monday.

In the House of Commons, that afternoon, Mr. Baldwin rose, to answer Mr. Attlee's question as to whether he had any further information to give to the House.

Mr. Baldwin : "I regret I am not in a position to add anything to-day, but I hope to make a statement to-morrow."

Mr. Attlee : "May I ask him whether he can give us a good hope that in the statement to-morrow he will realize the anxiety which is continually increasing so long as this matter is not dealt with ?"

Mr. Baldwin : "I can assure the right honourable gentleman and the House that no one realizes that more than I do."

Mr. Bellenger : "May I ask the Prime Minister whether he is aware that grave financial inconvenience is being caused to many subjects in this country by the delay in coming to a decision, and will the Prime Minister kindly suggest to His Majesty" (cries of "Oh !") "the necessity of coming to an early decision ?"

Mr. Baldwin : "I can assure Mr. Bellenger that that has not escaped me."

Parliament was now anxious to bring the matter to an end.

When the formal business of the House was over the Cabinet met for the second time that day. Here the Ministers received reports from the Dominion Governments on the decision which had already been communicated to them. They also made arrangements for the legislation that would have to follow the statement which the Premier had promised to make to Parliament the next day.

The Duke of York returned to 145 Piccadilly from Fort Belvedere shortly before nine o'clock that night.

Near 9 p.m. the Prime Minister, Sir John Simon and Mr. Walter Monckton, K.C., arrived at No. 10 Downing Street within a minute of each other. Shortly afterwards Sir John Simon and Mr. Monckton left together in Sir John's car, returning a little later. In the interval Mr. M. MacDonald arrived. It was at 11.20 when Mr. Monckton left No. 10, but he returned once more at 11.50 and stayed until 12.15, when he left Sir John Simon still in conference with the Premier. It was not until half an hour after midnight that Sir John,

F   79

in company with Sir Edward Peacock, left Downing Street.

When the door of No. 10 closed on Sir John Simon everything was ready for the next day's drama. Newspapers went to press that night with the news that abdication was almost certain.

Chapter VII

MR. BALDWIN TELLS THE STORY

THE WORLD AWOKE ON THURSDAY morning to find the headlines predicting abdication. It became the one important topic of the day. Barely had the morning crowds proceeded to their work when the leading figures in the drama were once again moving about the scene. Whitehall became the centre of universal interest.

By 10 o'clock the King's three brothers were at Fort Belvedere. At 10.45 Sir John Simon was once more closeted with the Prime Minister. They were joined later by Mr. Ramsay MacDonald, the Lord Privy Seal, and Mr. Malcolm MacDonald, the Dominions Secretary. Within the hour Mr. Walter

Monckton, K.C., and Sir Edward Peacock arrived at No. 10, having first called at Buckingham Palace. By noon the preliminaries were over and Sir John Simon, with Mr. Monckton, K.C., left the Home Office to visit the King and his brothers at Fort Belvedere.

Throughout the day Whitehall remained a scene of great animation and in the thick of the comings and goings Mr. Baldwin was seen to leave for the Commons a little before a quarter to three.

It had been announced that Mr. Baldwin would make a statement that day and interest was roused to fever pitch by a radio announcement that his speech would be reported at 4 p.m. Great crowds began to collect in Whitehall and the precincts of the Houses of Parliament. There was a full attendance of members long before the opening of the day's session. All the galleries were packed. Diplomats, peers and distinguished visitors crowded the galleries. Members overflowed into all parts of the Chamber. The Speaker took the chair and called the first question after the House had said prayers.

Fifty-one routine questions were put and an

impatient House sat through the Ministerial replies.[1]
Then Mr. Baldwin rose, went to the Bar of the
House and bowed low to the Speaker. In one of
the tensest scenes ever witnessed in an English
Parliament he began the proceedings.

"A message from His Majesty the King, signed
by His Majesty's own hand," he said.

As Mr. Baldwin walked towards the Speaker,
holding the fateful document—three foolscap sheets,
stamped with a red seal—he stopped to bow and
then continued until, with another bow, he handed
the document to the Speaker.

Those members who were covered bared their
heads as Captain Fitzroy, the Speaker, began to
read the words written on the pages which he
now held in his trembling hand.

AFTER LONG AND ANXIOUS CON-
SIDERATION, I HAVE DETERMINED TO
RENOUNCE THE THRONE TO WHICH I
SUCCEEDED ON THE DEATH OF MY

[1] Although the House was seething with excitement as it
anticipated the speech of the Premier, the procedure was strictly
adhered to. Parliament always adheres to precedent. After Mr.
Speaker has taken the chair at 2.45 p.m. the chaplain says prayers.
Questions are then called at 3 p.m. (and if a new member is to take
his seat he does so immediately after questions). Only then can the
legislative business begin.

FATHER, AND I AM NOW COMMUNI-
CATING THIS MY FINAL AND IRREVO-
CABLE DECISION. REALIZING AS I DO
THE GRAVITY OF THIS STEP, I CAN ONLY
HOPE THAT I SHALL HAVE THE UNDER-
STANDING OF MY PEOPLE IN THE
DECISION I HAVE TAKEN AND THE
REASONS WHICH HAVE LED ME TO TAKE
IT.

I WILL NOT ENTER NOW INTO MY
PRIVATE FEELINGS, BUT I WOULD BEG
THAT IT SHOULD BE REMEMBERED THAT
THE BURDEN WHICH CONSTANTLY RESTS
UPON THE SHOULDERS OF A SOVEREIGN
IS SO HEAVY THAT IT CAN ONLY BE
BORNE IN CIRCUMSTANCES DIFFERENT
FROM THOSE IN WHICH I NOW FIND
MYSELF.

I CONCEIVE THAT I AM NOT OVER-
LOOKING THE DUTY THAT RESTS ON
ME TO PLACE IN THE FOREFRONT THE
PUBLIC INTEREST WHEN I DECLARE
THAT I AM CONSCIOUS THAT I CAN NO
LONGER DISCHARGE THIS HEAVY TASK
WITH EFFICIENCY OR WITH SATISFAC-

TION TO MYSELF. I HAVE ACCORDINGLY
THIS MORNING EXECUTED AN INSTRU-
MENT OF ABDICATION IN THE TERMS
FOLLOWING :

"I, EDWARD VIII, OF GREAT
BRITAIN, IRELAND AND THE BRITISH
DOMINIONS BEYOND THE SEAS, KING,
EMPEROR OF INDIA, DO HEREBY
DECLARE MY IRREVOCABLE DETER-
MINATION TO RENOUNCE THE
THRONE FOR MYSELF AND FOR MY
DESCENDANTS AND MY DESIRE THAT
EFFECT SHOULD BE GIVEN TO
THIS INSTRUMENT OF ABDICATION
IMMEDIATELY.

"IN TOKEN WHEREOF I HAVE HERE-
UNTO SET MY HAND THIS 10TH DAY
OF DECEMBER, 1936, IN THE PRESENCE
OF THE WITNESSES WHOSE SIGNA-
TURES ARE SUBSCRIBED.

(Signed)   EDWARD R.I."

MY EXECUTION OF THIS INSTRUMENT
HAS BEEN WITNESSED BY MY THREE

BROTHERS, THEIR ROYAL HIGHNESSES THE DUKE OF YORK, THE DUKE OF GLOUCESTER AND THE DUKE OF KENT.

I DEEPLY APPRECIATE THE SPIRIT WHICH HAS ACTUATED THE APPEALS WHICH HAVE BEEN MADE TO ME TO TAKE A DIFFERENT DECISION, AND I HAVE, BEFORE REACHING MY FINAL DETERMINATION, MOST FULLY PONDERED OVER THEM. BUT MY MIND IS MADE UP. MOREOVER, FURTHER DELAY CANNOT BUT BE MOST INJURIOUS TO THE PEOPLES WHOM I HAVE TRIED TO SERVE AS PRINCE OF WALES AND AS KING AND WHOSE FUTURE HAPPINESS AND PROSPERITY ARE THE CONSTANT WISH OF MY HEART.

I TAKE MY LEAVE OF THEM IN THE CONFIDENT HOPE THAT THE COURSE WHICH I HAVE THOUGHT IT RIGHT TO FOLLOW IS THAT WHICH IS BEST FOR THE STABILITY OF THE THRONE AND EMPIRE AND THE HAPPINESS OF MY PEOPLES. I AM DEEPLY SENSIBLE OF THE CONSIDERATION WHICH THEY

HAVE ALWAYS EXTENDED TO ME, BOTH BEFORE AND AFTER MY ACCESSION TO THE THRONE, AND WHICH I KNOW THEY WILL EXTEND IN FULL MEASURE TO MY SUCCESSOR.

I AM MOST ANXIOUS THAT THERE SHOULD BE NO DELAY OF ANY KIND IN GIVING EFFECT TO THE INSTRUMENT WHICH I HAVE EXECUTED, AND THAT ALL NECESSARY STEPS SHOULD BE TAKEN IMMEDIATELY TO SECURE THAT MY LAWFUL SUCCESSOR, MY BROTHER, HIS ROYAL HIGHNESS THE DUKE OF YORK, SHOULD ASCEND THE THRONE.

EDWARD R.I.

INSTRUMENT OF ABDICATION

       I, Edward the Eighth, of Great
Britain, Ireland, and the British Dominions
beyond the Seas, King, Emperor of India, do
hereby declare My irrevocable determination
to renounce the Throne for Myself and for
My descendants, and My desire that effect
should be given to this Instrument of
Abdication immediately.

       In token whereof I have hereunto set
My hand this tenth day of December, nineteen
hundred and thirty six, in the presence of
the witnesses whose signatures are subscribed.

SIGNED AT
FORT BELVEDERE
IN THE PRESENCE
OF

Edward RI

Albert

Henry.

George.

In deep silence Mr. Baldwin again stood up to move the motion :

"That His Majesty's most gracious Message be now considered."

He spoke deliberately, extempore, to a hushed House, never for one moment exhibiting a sign of nervousness. It was a tremendous moment for him, for he was to tell in full the story of how a King had decided to renounce his Throne. And he was asking Parliament to accept a position which had resulted from a development in which he, almost unaided, had played a leading part. These are his words :

"No more grave message has ever been received by Parliament, and no more difficult, I may almost say repugnant, task has ever been imposed upon a Prime Minister. I would ask the House, which I know will not be without sympathy for me in my position to-day, to remember that in this last week I have had but little time in which to compose a speech for delivery to-day, so I must tell what I have to tell truthfully, sincerely, and plainly, with no attempt to dress up or to adorn. I shall have little or nothing to say in the way of comment or criticism, or of praise or of blame. I think my best course to-day, and the one that the House would desire, is to tell them, so far as I can, what has passed between His Majesty and myself, and what led up to the present situation.

"I should like to say at the start that His Majesty, as Prince of Wales, has honoured me for many years with a friendship which I value, and I know that he would agree with me in saying to you that it was not only a friendship but, between man and man, a friendship of affection. I would like to tell the House that when we said 'Good-bye' on Tuesday night at Fort Belvedere we both knew, and felt, and said to each other that that friendship, so far from being impaired by the discussions of this last week, bound us more closely together than ever, and would last for life.

"Now, Sir, the House will want to know how it was that I had my first interview with His Majesty. I may say that His Majesty has been most generous in allowing me to tell the House the pertinent parts of the discussions which took place between us. As the House is aware, I had been ordered in August and September a complete rest which, owing to the kindness of my staff and the consideration of all my colleagues, I was able to enjoy to the full, and when October came, although I had been ordered to take a rest in that month, I felt that I could not in fairness to my work take a further holiday, and I came, as it were, on half-time before the middle of October and, for the first time since the beginning of August, was in a position to look into things.

"There were two things that disquieted me at that moment. There was coming to my office a vast volume of correspondence, mainly at that time from British subjects and American citizens of British origin in the United States of America, from some of the Dominions, and from this country, all expressing perturbation and uneasiness at what was then appearing in the American Press. I was aware also that there was, in the near future, a divorce case coming on, the results of which made me realize that possibly a difficult situation might arise later, and I felt that it was essential that someone should see His Majesty and warn him of the difficult situation that might arise later if occasion was given for a continuation of this kind of gossip and of criticism, and the danger that might come if that gossip and that criticism spread from the other side of the Atlantic to this country. I felt that in the circumstances there was only one man who could speak to him and talk the matter over with him, and that man was the Prime Minister. I felt doubly bound to do it by my duty, as I conceived it, to the country, and my duty to him not only as a counsellor, but

as a friend. I consulted, I am ashamed to say—
and they have forgiven me—none of my colleagues.

"I happened to be staying in the neighbourhood
of Fort Belvedere about the middle of October,
and I ascertained that His Majesty was leaving
his house on Sunday, October 18th, to entertain
a small shooting party at Sandringham, and that
he was leaving on the Sunday afternoon. I
telephoned from my friend's house on the Sunday
morning, and found that he had left earlier than
was expected. In those circumstances I communicated with him through his secretary, and
stated that I desired to see him—this is the first
and only occasion on which I was the one who
asked for an interview—that I desired to see
him, that the matter was urgent. I told him
what it was. I expressed my willingness to come
to Sandringham on Tuesday, the 20th, but I
said that I thought it wiser, if His Majesty thought
fit, to see me at Fort Belvedere, for I was anxious
that no one at that time should know of my visit,
and that at any rate our first talk should be in
complete privacy. The reply came from His
Majesty that he would motor back on the Monday,
19th October, to Fort Belvedere, and he would
see me on the Tuesday morning. And on the
Tuesday morning I saw him.

"Sir, I may say, before I proceed to the details
of the conversation, that an adviser to the Crown

can be of no possible service to his master unless he tells him at all times the truth as he sees it, whether that truth be welcome or not. And let me say here, as I may say several times before I finish, that during those talks, when I look back, there is nothing I have not told His Majesty of which I felt he ought to be aware—nothing. His Majesty's attitude all through has been—let me put it in this way : Never has he shown any sign of offence, of being hurt at anything I have said to him. The whole of our discussions have been carried out, as I have said, with an increase, if possible, of that mutual respect and regard in which we stood. I told His Majesty that I had two great anxieties—one the effect of a continuance of the kind of criticism that at that time was proceeding in the American Press, the effect it would have in the Dominions, and particularly in Canada, where it was widespread, the effect it would have in this country.

"That was the first anxiety. And then I reminded him of what I had often told him and his brothers in years past. The British Monarchy is a unique institution. The Crown in this country through the centuries has been deprived of many of its prerogatives, but to-day, while that is true, it stands for far more than it ever has done in its history. The importance of its integrity is, beyond all question, far greater than it has ever been, being as it is not only the last link of Empire that is left, but the guarantee in this country, so long as it exists in that integrity, against many evils that have affected and afflicted other countries. There is no man in this country, to whatever party he may belong, who would not subscribe to that. But while this feeling largely depends on the respect that has grown up in the last three generations for the Monarchy, it might not take so long, in face of the kind of criticisms to which it was being exposed, to lose that power far more rapidly than it was built up, and once lost, I doubt if anything could restore it.

"That was the basis of my talk on that aspect, and I expressed my anxiety and desire, that such criticism should not have cause to go on. I said that, in my view, no popularity in the long run would be weighed against the effect of such criticism. I told His Majesty that I for one had looked forward to his reign being a great reign in a new age—he has so many of the qualities necessary—and that I hoped we should be able to see our hopes realized. I told him I had come—naturally, I was his Prime Minister —but I wanted to talk it over with him as a friend to see if I could help him in this matter. Perhaps I am saying what I should not say here ; I have not asked him whether I might say this, but I will say it because I do not think he would mind, and I think it illustrates the basis on which our talks proceeded. He said to me, not once, but many times during those many, many hours we have had together, and especially towards the end, 'You and I must settle this matter together ; I will not have anyone interfering.'

"I then pointed out the danger of the divorce proceedings, that if a verdict was given in that case that left the matter in suspense for some time, that period of suspense might be dangerous, because then everyone would be talking, and when once the Press began, as it must begin some time in this country, a most difficult situation would arise for me, for him, and there might well be a danger which both he and I had seen all through this—I shall come to that later— and it was one of the reasons why he wanted to take this action quickly—that is, that there might be sides taken and factions grow up in this country in a matter where no faction ought ever to exist.

"It was on that aspect of the question that we talked for an hour, and I went away glad that the ice had been broken, because I knew that it had to be broken. For some little time we had no further meetings. I begged His Majesty to consider all that I had said. I said that I pressed him for no kind of answer, but would he consider everything I had said ? The next time I saw him

G 95

was on Monday, November 16. That was at Buckingham Palace. By that date the decree *nisi* had been pronounced in the divorce case. His Majesty had sent for me on that occasion. I had meant to see him later in the week, but he had sent for me first. I felt it my duty to begin the conversation, and I spoke to him for a quarter of an hour or twenty minutes on the question of marriage.

"Again, we must remember that the Cabinet had not been in this at all—I had reported to about four of my senior colleagues the conversation at Fort Belvedere. I saw the King on Monday, November 16, and I began by giving him my view of a possible marriage. I told him that I did not think that a particular marriage was one that would receive the approbation of the country. That marriage would have involved the lady becoming Queen. I did tell His Majesty once that I might be a remnant of the old Victorians, but that my worst enemy would not say of me that I did not know what the reaction of the English people would be to any particular course of action, and I told him that so far as they went, I was certain that that would be impracticable. I cannot go further into the details, but that was the substance. I pointed out to him that the position of the King's wife was different from the position of the wife of any other citizen in the country ; it was part of the price which the King has to pay. His wife becomes Queen ; the Queen becomes the Queen of the country ; and, therefore, in the choice of a Queen the voice of the people must be heard. It is the truth expressed in those lines that may come to your minds :

'His will is not his own ;
For he himself is subject to his birth,
He may not, as unvalued persons do,
Carve for himself ; for on his choice depends
The safety and the health of the whole State.[1]'

"Then His Majesty said to me—I have his permission to state this—that he wanted to tell me something that he had long wanted to tell me. He said, 'I am going to marry Mrs. Simpson, and I am prepared to go.' I said, 'Sir, that is most grievous news, and it is impossible for me to make any comment on it to-day.' He told the Queen that night ; he told the Duke of York and the Duke of Gloucester the next day, and the Duke of Kent, who was out of London, either on the Wednesday or the Thursday ; and for the rest of the week, so far as I know, he was considering that point.

"He sent for me again on Wednesday, November 25. In the meantime a suggestion had been

[1] *Hamlet*, Act I, Scene 3.

made to me that a possible compromise might be arranged to avoid those two possibilities that had been seen, first in the distance, and then approaching nearer and nearer. The compromise was that the King should marry, that Parliament should pass an Act enabling the lady to be the King's wife without the position of Queen ; and when I saw His Majesty on November 25 he asked me whether that proposition had been put to me, and I said yes. He asked me what I thought of it. I told him that I had not considered it. I said, 'I can give you no considered opinion.' If he asked me my first reaction informally, my first reaction was that Parliament would never pass such a Bill. But I said that, if he desired it I would examine it formally. He said he did so desire. Then I said, 'It will mean my putting that formally before the whole Cabinet, and communicating with the Prime Ministers of all Dominions, and was that his wish ?' He told me that it was. I said that I would do it.

"On December 2 the King asked me to go and see him. Again I had intended asking for an audience later that week, because such inquiries as I thought proper to make I had not completed. The inquiries had gone far enough to show that neither in the Dominions nor here would there be any prospect of such legislation being accepted. His Majesty asked me if I could answer his question. I gave him the reply that I was afraid it was impracticable for those reasons. I do want the House to realize this : His Majesty said he was not surprised at that answer. He took my answer with no question, and he never recurred to it again. I want the House to realize—because if you can put yourself in His Majesty's place, and you know what His Majesty's feelings are, and you know how glad you would have been had this been possible—that he behaved there as a great gentleman ; he said no more about it. The matter was closed. I never heard another word about it from him. That decision was, of course, a formal decision, and that was the only formal decision of any kind taken by the Cabinet until I come to the history of yesterday. When we had finished that conversation, I pointed out that the possible alternatives had been narrowed, and that it really had brought him into the position that he would be placed in a grievous situation between two conflicting loyalties in his own heart—either complete abandonment of the project on which his heart was set, and remaining as King, or doing as he intimated to me that he was prepared to do, in the talk which I have reported, going, and later on contracting that marriage, if it were possible. During the last days, from that day until now, that has been the struggle in which His Majesty has been engaged.

We had many talks, and always on the various aspects of this limited problem.

"The House must remember—it is difficult to realize—that His Majesty is not a boy, although he looks so young. We have all thought of him as our Prince, but he is a mature man, with wide and great experience of life and the world, and he always had before him three, nay, four, things, which in these conversations at all hours, he repeated again and again— That if he went, he would go with dignity. He would not allow a situation to arise in which he could not do that. He wanted to go with as little disturbance of his Ministers and his people as possible. He wished to go in circumstances that would make the succession of his brother as little difficult for his brother as possible ; and I may say that any idea to him of what might be called a King's party, was abhorrent. He stayed down at Fort Belvedere because he said that he was not coming to London while these things were in dispute, because of the cheering crowds. I honour and respect him for the way in which he behaved at that time.

"I have something here which, I think, will touch the House. It is a pencilled note, sent to me by His Majesty this morning, and I have his authority for reading it. It is just scribbled in pencil :

"'Duke of York. He and the King have

always been on the best of terms as brothers, and the King is confident that the Duke deserves and will receive the support of the whole Empire.'

I would say a word or two on the King's position. The King cannot speak for himself. The King has told us that he cannot carry, and does not see his way to carry, these almost intolerable burdens of kingship without a woman at his side, and we know that. This crisis, if I may use the word, has arisen now rather than later from that very frankness of His Majesty's character which is one of his many attractions. It would have been perfectly possible for His Majesty not to have told me of this at the date when he did, and not to have told me for some months to come. But he realized the damage that might be done in the interval by gossip, rumours, and talk, and he made that declaration to me when he did, on purpose to avoid what he felt might be dangerous, not only here, but throughout the Empire, to the moral force of the Crown which we are all determined to sustain.

"He told me his intentions, and he has never wavered from them. I want the House to understand that. He felt it his duty to take into his anxious consideration all the representations that his advisers might give him, and not until he had fully considered them did he make public his decision. There has been no kind of conflict in this matter. My efforts during these last days have been directed, as have the efforts of those most closely round him, in trying to help him to make the choice which he has not made ; and we have failed. The King has made his decision to take this moment to send this Gracious Message because of his confident hope that by that he will preserve the unity of this country, and of the whole Empire, and avoid those factious differences which might so easily have arisen.

"It is impossible, unfortunately, to avoid talking to some extent to-day about one's self. These last days have been days of great strain, but it was a great comfort to me, and I hope it will be to the House, when I was assured before I left him on Tuesday night, by that intimate circle that was with him at the Fort that evening, that I had left nothing undone that I could have done to move him from the decision at which he had arrived, and which he has communicated to us. While there is not a soul among us who will not regret this from the bottom of his heart, there is not a soul here to-day that wants to judge. We are not judges. He has announced his decision. He has told us what he wants us to do, and I think we must close our ranks, and do it.

"At a later stage this evening I shall ask leave

to bring in the necessary Bill so that it may be read the first time, printed, and made available to members. It will be available in the Vote Office as soon as the House has ordered the Bill to be printed. The House will meet to-morrow at the usual time, 11 o'clock, when we shall take the second reading and the remaining stages of the Bill. It is very important that it should be passed into law to-morrow, and I shall put on the Order Paper to-morrow a motion to take Private Members' time, and to suspend the Four o'Clock Rule.

"I have only two other things to say. The House will forgive me for saying now something which I should have said a few minutes ago. I have told them of the circumstances under which I am speaking, and they have been very generous and sympathetic. Yesterday morning, when the Cabinet received the King's final and definite answer officially, they passed a Minute, and in accordance with it I sent a message to His Majesty, which he has been good enough to permit me to read to the House, with his reply.

" 'Mr. Baldwin, with his humble duty to the King.

" 'This morning Mr. Baldwin reported to the Cabinet his interview with Your Majesty yesterday, and informed his colleagues that Your Majesty then communicated to him informally Your firm and definite intention to renounce the Throne.

" 'The Cabinet received this statement of Your Majesty's intention with profound regret, and wished Mr. Baldwin to convey to Your Majesty immediately the unanimous feeling of Your Majesty's servants.

" 'Ministers are reluctant to believe that Your Majesty's resolve is irrevocable, and still venture to hope that before Your Majesty pronounces any formal decision Your Majesty may be pleased to reconsider an intention which must so deeply distress and so vitally affect all Your Majesty's subjects.

" 'Mr. Baldwin is at once communicating with the Dominion Prime Ministers for the purpose of letting them know that Your Majesty has now made to him the informal intimation of Your Majesty's intention.'

"His Majesty's reply was received last night.

" 'The King has received the Prime Minister's letter of the 9th December, 1936, informing him of the views of the Cabinet.

" 'His Majesty has given the matter his further consideration, but regrets that he is unable to alter his decision.'

My last words on that subject are that I am convinced that where I have failed no one could have succeeded. His mind was made up, and those who know His Majesty best will know what that means.

"This House to-day is a theatre which is being watched by the whole world. Let us conduct ourselves with that dignity which His Majesty is showing in this hour of his trial. Whatever our regret at the contents of the message, let us fulfil his wish, do what he asks, and do it with speed. Let no word be spoken to-day that the utterer of that word may regret in days to come, let no word be spoken that causes pain to any soul, and let us not forget to-day the revered and beloved figure of Queen Mary, what all this time has meant to her, and think of her when we have to speak, if speak we must, during this debate. We have, after all, as the guardians of democracy in this little island to see that we do our work to maintain the integrity of that democracy, and of the monarchy which, as I said at the beginning of my speech, is now the sole link of our whole Empire, and the guardian of our freedom. Let us look forward and remember our country and the trust reposed by our country in this, the House of Commons, and let us rally behind the new King—(Hon. Members : 'Hear hear')—stand behind him, and help him ; and let us hope that, whatever the country may have suffered by what we are passing through, it may soon be repaired, and that we may take what steps we can in trying to make this country a better country for all the people in it."

Mr. Baldwin resumed his seat amid a roar of cheers. This had been his day. The mantle of greatness had fallen upon him. His speech will always dominate the proceedings of the Parliament which considered the Abdication. The form of his speech was marked by classic simplicity. High tragedy was the note of the tale he had had to tell. He had revealed himself as a man who had handled a delicate question with tact and skill surpassing expectations.

There was nothing further to add, and yet something was expected of Mr. Attlee, who rose and said :

"Mr. Speaker. In view of the grave and important message which has been received from His Majesty, I would ask you whether it would not be desirable to suspend the sitting till, say, six o'clock, in order that members may give it due consideration ?"

To which the Speaker replied :

"If it is the wish of the House, I am prepared

to suspend the sitting until six o'clock, and to resume the chair at that hour."

The sitting was accordingly suspended at 4.33 p.m., and members flocked into the lobbies, not to discuss the Abdication of King Edward VIII, but a notable speech and the triumph of Mr. Stanley Baldwin.

Chapter VIII

THE OPPOSITION HAS A SAY

DURING THE ADJOURNMENT EXCITED members poured into the lobbies to discuss the sensation. They overflowed into the outer corridors where a great crowd of visitors were vainly endeavouring to interview their representatives. Members of The Parliamentary Labour Party gathered in Room 14 to decide their attitude in the light of the facts which had now been revealed. Mr. Attlee, the leader, outlined the speech he proposed to make on the resumption, and this was generally accepted, although Mr. Aneurin Bevan and a few others raised objections.

When the House reassembled at six o'clock, the Speaker called first on Mr. Attlee, who said :

"This occasion does not, in my view, call for long and eloquent speeches. My words will be few and simple. We have all heard with profound concern the message from His Majesty the King. The Prime Minister has related to us the course of events that have led up to this momentous act. The King has decided that he can no longer continue on the Throne. The whole country will receive the news with deep sorrow, and his subjects in these islands and throughout the British Dominions beyond the seas will feel a sense of personal loss. I am certain that, throughout these anxious days, he has had the sympathy of all, in the tragic dilemma with which he has been faced. That sympathy is due not only to the nature of the issue, involving as it does the strongest human emotions, but to the personal affection which he has inspired in his people. No British Monarch has been so well known by his subjects. The people not only in this country but throughout the Commonwealth and the Empire, have seen in him, not a remote Ruler, but a man who was personally acquainted with many of them and had visited the places where they live.

"For many years, as the Prince of Wales, he served his country. He shared its joys and sorrows in the dark days of the War and in time of peace. It seems but the other day that he was called upon to take the greater responsibilities of Sovereign over a quarter of the peoples of the world. We all know his personal charm, his courage, and his ready sympathy with suffering. We, on these benches, can never forget how he felt for the miners in their time of trial, and how he showed his deep interest in the unemployed and the people of the distressed areas. Now he has had to make a difficult choice. Powerful personal and human considerations have conflicted with the obligations and responsibilities of his high calling. I am sure that all of us have been trying to think of some way by which this conflict could be resolved. We realized the grave objections to every course, and we hoped it would not come to abdication ; but the King has made his decision. He has resolved to abide by it, and we can do no other than accept it.

"The wish of all his people will be that he may have a long and happy life. We can all appreciate the strain which these events have placed on the Prime Minister, and he is entitled to our sympathy. The country has received a severe shock. It will take time to recover. The position of anyone who, in these days of pressing problems at home and abroad, is called upon to accept the Throne in these unprecedented circumstances, is obviously one of very great strain. It will be the endeavour of all of us to do what we may to lighten that burden. I would like to express on behalf of myself and my colleagues our deepest sympathy with Queen Mary and the other Members of the Royal Family."

Mr. Attlee was followed by the leader of the Opposition Liberals, Sir Archibald Sinclair :

"The whole country and the Empire have been passing through days of stress and tension, and the climax to which events have now marched has aroused in all of us the deepest feelings of grief and frustration. We are bound to our King not only by formal and solemn ties, by our oaths of allegiance and by our recognition of the Crown as the link which unites all the peoples of the Empire, but also by those closer and more personal links which the Leader of the Opposition has so simply and so eloquently described, and which the King has forged between himself and his people—people of all classes, of all creeds and of all races in every part of his Dominions—during nearly a quarter of a century of Royal service. The rupture of those ties is profoundly painful to us all. It must be most painful to those right hon. gentlemen who, during these brief months of his Reign have been his Ministers and confidential advisers ; above all, to the Prime Minister, his closest and most intimate adviser, who deserves our sympathy, and to-day also our gratitude for the grave but clear and moving statement which it was his melancholy duty to make to us this afternoon.

"Let us also gratefully and respectfully acclaim the political wisdom which His Majesty has shown in discountenancing any attempt to divide the country on the issues to which his proposed marriage gave rise. It is in large measure due to His Majesty's wise and strong restraint, and to his recognition of the supremacy of Parliament and the constitutional responsibility of Ministers, that the Crown has not become involved in our political controversies, but remains above and aloof from them.

"The Leader of the Opposition spoke of the earnestness and the anxiety with which all of us have been exploring the possibility of finding some means by which this conflict could be resolved. The Prime Minister referred to the possibility of a Morganatic Marriage Bill ; I think it is only right to tell the House that I could not have supported it. It is not only the law of our country but it is also, I believe, a sound, healthy and essential element in the monarchical principle itself, that the lady whom the King marries must become Queen and share with him, before the whole people, the glorious burden of sovereignty. Such a Bill would, moreover, under the Statute of Westminster, have had to pass through all the Parliaments of the United Kingdom and the Dominions, before it could have become valid in this country or in any of the Dominions, and the attempt to do so would have involved the Throne in prolonged controversy which would have gravely impaired its prestige and dignity. In my judgment the Government had no option but to reject the proposal.

"No man deserves more the generous sympathy and support of the British people at this time than the devoted brother and loyal subject of the present King, whose duty it will be to succeed him on the Throne. He has enjoyed some, but not all, of the opportunities which long tenure of the dignity of Prince of Wales usually affords the Heir to the Throne, of becoming well known to the people of this country; but he has worked hard for many good causes. Thousands of young people who have shared with him the unconventional delights of camp life can testify to his good comradeship and democratic instincts. None will doubt his sincerity and high sense of public duty, and all will welcome to the Throne that gracious lady his wife, who was born a commoner but has won the hearts of the British people by showing a clear and just conception of Royal duty and opportunity in a democratic country.

"Grief-stricken as we are to-day, it is our duty to face the future with clear eyes and firm resolve. Any prolongation of the crisis would be fraught with peril. For my own part, I doubt whether under any system of Government a crisis of this gravity could be solved with as little disturbance to the body politic as under our system of constitutional monarchy. This, at any rate, is certain, that the prompt action which the King himself has enjoined upon us will best serve the dignity of the Throne, the reputation of our Parliamentary institutions and the happiness, prosperity, and peace of the British people."

After Sir Archibald Sinclair had resumed his seat the debate could only be carried on by those who had expressed dissent during the days when the issue had lain in suspense.

A tense House saw Mr. Churchill rise in his place and heard the Speaker call his name. In the dim light of the Chamber members leaned forward to hear what he had to say. They remembered that on Monday when he had risen to put a supplementary question to the Premier they had expressed their disapproval in no uncertain terms. What would be Mr. Churchill's attitude now? Would he once more wax eloquent with indignation and wrath? Or would he bow to the inevitable and state his concurrence with that which had been done and which now seemed to be irrevocable? Members knew that he had pondered the question during the interval. They knew him, too, as one of the real orators of the House, one who carried into these strange and dramatic times the traditions of the giants of the nineteenth century.

In the galleries, crowded almost to suffocation, peers grown old in the service of the State cupped their ears the better to catch his words. An indefinite buzz flitted over the visitors' galleries, and the words, "Mister Churchill" passed from lip to lip. Diplomats, wondering at this strange scene, leaned forward, and in the Press gallery, parliamentary reporters got ready for drama.

Such scenes are known but rarely to the House of Commons and the men of the Press prepared to rush the speech to their papers, Mr. Churchill said:

"Nothing is more certain or more obvious than that recrimination or controversy at this time would be not only useless, but harmful and wrong. What is done, is done. What has been done, or left undone, belongs to history, and to history, so far as I am concerned, it shall be left.

I will, therefore, make two observations only. The first is this : It is clear from what we have been told this afternoon that there was at no time any constitutional issue between the King and his Ministers, or between the King and Parliament. The supremacy of Parliament over the Crown ; the duty of the Sovereign to act in accordance with the advice of his Ministers ; neither of those was ever at any moment in question. Supporting my right hon. friend, the leader of the Liberal Party, I venture to say that no Sovereign has ever conformed more strictly or more faithfully to the letter and spirit of the Constitution than his present Majesty. In fact, he has voluntarily made a sacrifice for the peace and strength of his Realm which go far beyond the bounds required by the law and the Constitution. This is my first observation.

"My second is this : I have, throughout, pleaded for time ; anyone can see how grave would have been the evils of protracted controversy. On the other hand it was, in my view, our duty to endure these evils, even at serious inconvenience, if there was any hope that time would bring a solution. Whether there was any hope or not is a mystery which, at the present time, it is impossible to resolve. Time was also important from another point of view. It was essential that there should be no room for aspersions, after the event, that the King had been hurried to his decision. I believe that, if this decision had been taken last week, it could not have been declared that it was an unhurried decision, so far as the King himself was concerned, but now I accept wholeheartedly what the Prime Minister has proved, namely, that the decision taken this week has been taken by His Majesty freely, voluntarily and spontaneously, in his own time and in his own way. As I have been looking at this matter, as is well known, from an angle different from that of most hon. members, I thought it my duty to place this fact also upon record.

"That is all I have to say upon the disputable part of this matter, but I hope the House will bear with me for a minute or two, because it was my duty as Home Secretary, more than a quarter of a century ago, to stand beside his Majesty and proclaim his style and titles at his investiture as Prince of Wales amid the sunlit battlements of Caernarvon Castle, and ever since then he has honoured me here, and also in war-time, with his personal kindness and, I may even say, friendship. I should have been ashamed if, in my independent and unofficial position, I had not cast about for every lawful means, even the most forlorn, to keep him on the Throne of his fathers, to which he only recently succeeded amid the hopes and prayers of all. In this Prince there were discerned qualities of courage, of simplicity, of sympathy and, above all, of sincerity, qualities rare and precious which might have made his Reign glorious in the annals of this ancient Monarchy. It is the acme of tragedy that these very virtues should, in the private sphere, have led only to this melancholy and bitter conclusion. But, although our hopes to-day are withered, still I will assert that his personality will not go down uncherished to future ages, that it will be particularly remembered in the homes of his poorer subjects, and that they will ever wish from the bottoms of their hearts for his private peace and happiness, and for the happiness of those who are dear to him.

"I must say one word more, and I say it especially to those here and out of doors—and do not underrate their numbers—who are most poignantly afflicted by what has occurred. Danger gathers upon our path. We cannot afford—we have no right—to look back. We must look forward ; we must obey the exhortation of the Prime Minister to look forward. The stronger the advocate of monarchical principle a man may be, the more zealously must he now endeavour to fortify the Throne, and to give His Majesty's successor that strength which can only come from the love of a united nation and Empire."

When Mr. Churchill sat down a hum of excitement pervaded the House. From his first words all who had listened to that speech—excellent in phrase and lofty in sentiment—knew that he had faced the inevitable with courage and nobility. Visitors had been prepared for much, but none had expected such magnanimity as that which this orator had breathed into his utterance. So far as Mr. Churchill was concerned the crisis had been resolved. It was finished.

But the end had not yet come to the debate. It was noticed that as Mr. Churchill resumed his seat two or three more members of the Opposition had risen to their feet, eager to catch the Speaker's eye.

"Mr. Maxton," called the Speaker.

Mr. Maxton flicked a heavy strand of hair from his forehead, and began to express the attitude of his group on this momentous question :

"I rise to say a few words on this unprecedented situation in which the House of Commons finds itself to-day, and I realize that I am speaking in a House in which an overwhelming proportion of the membership is under feelings of very strong emotion. I respect these emotions, although I do not entirely share them. The monarchical institutions of this land date back to very early times, and by many are regarded as sacrosanct and everlasting. I share with others in this House the human sympathies that go out to His Majesty as a man confronted with the difficulties with which he as a man has been confronted in these recent weeks. I share the same human sympathies with the Prime Minister, who has had to shoulder a task which few if any of the occupants of his office have ever had to shoulder before, and, in the nature of the case, has had to shoulder it alone. The decisions that he has made are, I believe, in strict accordance with his Conservative principles, on which he has been chosen as the leader of this country in the House of Commons, and, therefore, I make no criticism of them whatever. But I do say that, in the very nature of the monarchical institutions on an hereditary basis, circumstances of this kind were bound to arise, and they have arisen now in conditions which have created very grave difficulties for this country and for the Empire over the seas.

"It is a question whether now this House will not be prepared to look at this particular political problem that has been forced upon our attention to-day as a practical political problem, one among many that intelligent men in the twentieth century must confront, recognizing that the problems of our age cannot be met and solved with the ideas and the institutions which have come down to us from earlier times. We are living in a new kind of world, with new kinds of problems, and the institutions that date back centuries, however much reverence they may inspire because of their ancient origin and the traditions and associations that have become attached to them over the centuries, are not necessarily the institutions which can cope with the problems of modern times. We therefore intend, however it may be against the general run of opinion in this House, to take strongly the view that the lesson of the past few days, and of this day in particular, is that the monarchical institution has now outlived its usefulness. [Hon. Members : "No."] The happenings of the past few days have only indicated the grave perils that confront a country that has as its centralizing, unifying figure an hereditary personality who at any time may break under the force of the circumstances that gather round about him. We hope to take the opportunity given us, when steps are being taken to make good the evil and injury that have already been done to try to persuade this House now to face the situation with the idea in their minds that for the future Great Britain and its allied

countries across the seas shall become, among
other advanced countries in the world, one of
the republican nations."

Then Colonel Josiah Wedgwood made amends
for his intercession at the onset of the crisis :[1]

"I put a Motion on the Paper, and I do not
regret it ; but, after the sincere and admirable
speech of the Prime Minister, that Motion is
dead. I could have wished that the King had
been allowed to live here married, happy, and
King, but he has wished otherwise. A thousand
years hence, perhaps, we shall be liberal enough
to allow such a thing ; it is too early now. He
has been very kind to me and to a great many
people throughout this Empire personally known
to him, and I think we may all wish him a happy
life there, if not here. The right hon. Gentleman
has made it perfectly clear that, in spite of what
I wished, and many others wished, there were
really only two alternatives—to continue lonely,
disappointed, bitter, ruling the Empire, or else
to do what he has done, to throw up royalty
and remain a man. We shall all commend him
for that choice of the two, for nothing could
have been worse than a Kingdom ruled by a man
with a grievance, partly hostile to every Minister
who had put him in the dilemma—[Hon.

[1] See page 45.

MEMBERS : "No !"]—collecting round him false friends—[HON. MEMBERS : "No !"]—collecting round him those who would use the King's feelings against the Ministry and against the Constitution. That would be an alternative which everyone must have seen ahead of us, the most dreadful alternative. To-morrow we shall take a new Oath of Allegiance. There will be no non-jurors this time, because it is by the King's wish that we take it. There will be no non-jurors below the Gangway, no non-jurors through-out the country. There will be, I would say, millions of people with aching hearts. They will carry on for England. They will take that oath because he wished it, and, if they sometimes raise their glass to the King across the water, who shall blame them ?"

The gallery thought that the last had been said, but they had not noticed Mr. William Gallacher, who more than once had risen to his feet. There was a mutter of surprise as they now heard Mr. Speaker call his name. Mr. Gallacher, standing stockily below the gangway, dropped his papers on his seat, and said :

"I would like just to remark that the concluding sentence of the right hon. Gentleman the Member for Epping (Mr. Churchill) happened to be the first note that I have in my hand. Danger lies before us, and it is going to be very bad if we close our eyes to that fact. It is very nice to hear right hon. Members talking about the necessity for all standing together, but how was it possible that such a crisis as has arisen should come upon us? The King and Mrs. Simpson do not live in a vacuum. Sinister processes are continually at work.

"I would direct your attention to the fact that the Prime Minister told us that he was approached about a morganatic marriage, but he did not tell us who approached him. He told us that, when he went to the King later, the King asked him if he had been approached on this matter. It is obvious that forces were operating, advising and encouraging what was going on. It is a year since I heard about Mrs. Simpson. Perhaps it is the same with other Members. No one paid very much attention to Mrs. Simpson or to what she was doing until more and more difficulties arose in Europe, and then there was a move for a decree *nisi*. This is not something decided on by the King and Mrs. Simpson on her own. I want to make it understood, if I possibly can, that we have here not an issue between the King and Parliament, for Parliament has never been consulted from beginning to end— interviews, secret and otherwise, but Parliament not consulted and the forces operating, two forces fighting with one another on this issue, as they have been fighting continually on every important issue that has come on foreign policy. I am concerned with the working class. I see terrible dangers arising. There is not an hon. Member here who, if he asks himself the question, believes that this finishes the crisis and that the forces which have been operating behind this will now stop. There is victory for one group at the moment, but they will not stop. The forces will go on.

"I want to draw attention to the fact that Mrs. Simpson has a social set, and every Member of the Cabinet knows that the social set of Mrs. Simpson is closely identified with a certain foreign Government and the Ambassador of that foreign Government. It is common knowledge, and round about this issue is the issue that is continually arising when other Debates come on. I say it is not an issue between the King and Parliament. It is an issue between two groups which are fighting continually for domination, and it is a thousand pities that the Labour movement should show any signs of falling into the trap. The only hope for the working class is that the Labour Movement should adopt an independent policy and pursue it against these groups, accept the proposal of the hon. Member for Bridgeton (Mr. Maxton) and finish with it all. No one can go out before the people of the country and give any justification for clinging to the Monarchy. You all know it. You will not be able, no matter what you do, to repair the damage that has been done to the Monarchical institution. If you allow things to go on as they are going, you will encourage factions to grow, and factions will grow, of a dangerous and desperate character, so far as the mass of the people are concerned. I appeal to the Labour movement to take strong, determined action to arouse the people of the country to the urgent need of uniting all their forces for peace and progress in face of the dangers that lie in their path—the very terrible dangers that are bound to confront us in the very near future."

Came Mr. George Buchanan's turn. He spoke the last words of opposition :

"I feel that I ought to express my own view and go a step farther than my hon. Friend the member for Bridgeton (Mr. Maxton). I should not be honest if I did not do so. I have listened to more cant and humbug than I have ever listened to in my life. I have heard praise of the King which was not felt sincerely in any quarter of the House. I go further. Who has not heard the tittle-tattle and gossip that is going about ? If he had not voluntarily stepped from the Throne, everyone knows that the same people in the House who pay lip service to him would have poured out scorn, abuse and filth. Some months ago we opposed the Civil List. To-morrow we shall take the same line. I have no doubt that you will go on praising the next King as you have praised this one. You will go on telling about his wonderful qualities. If he is a tenth as good as you say, why are you not keeping him ? Why is everyone wanting to unload him ? Because you know he is a weak creature. You want to get rid of him and you are taking the step to-day.

"The great tragedy of it is this : If an ordinary workman had been in this mess, everyone in the House of Commons would have been ashamed of him. You would have refused him benefit. You would have ill-treated him. Look at the Minister of Labour sneering at collusive action. [Hon. Members : "No, no !"] Everyone knows it. The whole Law Courts were set at defiance for this man. A divorce case was taken when every-one of you know it was a breaking of the law. What are you talking nonsense about ? The law is desecrated. The Law Courts are thrust aside. There is an association which everyone of you know is collusive action. If a little boy in Wales leaves his mother to get 7s. extra, he has to stand the jeers and taunts of a miserable Minister of Labour. Talk to me about fairness, about decency, about equality! You are setting aside your laws for a rich, pampered Royalty. The next set will be pampered too. You will lie and praise them and try to laud them above ordinary men. Instead of having the ordinary frailties that all of us have, they will have this additional one, of being surrounded with a set of flunkeys who refuse to let them know the truth as others do. To-morrow I will willingly take the step of going out and saying it is time the people ceased to trust those folk, but only trusted their own power and their own elected authority."

Then Captain Sir Ian Fraser closed the discussion :

"I feel sure that the House and the country will feel that any degree to which we can contribute towards avoiding controversy will be for the good of the Realm. I only want to say two things, not in any representative capacity but as an old soldier. No group in the community enjoys to a greater degree the understanding, the sympathy and the good will of His Majesty than ex-Service men. I am certain that they will feel not merely that they have lost one who has worked for them for a quarter of a century, but a personal friend. But no group has a deeper sense of the importance of stability and strength at difficult times. I feel certain that their loyalty to the Crown and their help to the new King will be unbounded and will be given in the greatest possible measure that lies in their power."

The motion that "the King's Message be now considered" was put and agreed to, and leave was given to bring in a Bill to give effect to His Majesty's Declaration of Abdication. This was read a first time and the House adjourned.

The text of the Abdication Bill, issued that evening, was as follows :

Whereas his Majesty by his royal message of the tenth day of December in this present year has been pleased to declare that he is irrevocably determined to renounce the Throne for himself and his descendants and has for that purpose executed the instrument of abdication set out in the schedule to this Act, and has signified his desire that effect thereto should be given immediately ;

And whereas following upon the communication to his Dominions of his Majesty's said declaration and desire, the Dominion of Canada, pursuant to the provisions of Section Four of the Statute of Westminster, 1931, has requested and consented to the enactment of this Act, and the Commonwealth of Australia, the Dominion of New Zealand, and the Union of South Africa have assented thereto :

Be it therefore enacted by the King's most excellent Majesty, by and with the advice and consent of the Lords spiritual and temporal and Commons, in this present Parliament assembled and by the authority of the same, as follows :

1—(1) Immediately upon the Royal Assent being signified to this Act the instrument of abdication executed by his present Majesty on the tenth day of December, 1936, set out in the schedule to this Act shall have effect, and thereupon his Majesty shall cease to be King and there shall be a demise of the Crown and accordingly the member of the Royal Family then next in succession to the Throne shall succeed thereto and to all the rights, privileges and dignities thereunto belonging.

(2) His Majesty, his issue, if any, and the descendants of that issue, shall not after his

Majesty's abdication have any right, title or interest in or to the succession to the throne, and Section One of the Act of Settlement shall be construed accordingly.

(3) The Royal Marriages Act, 1772, shall not apply to his Majesty after his abdication nor to the issue, if any, of his Majesty or the descendants of that issue.

2—This Act may be cited as his Majesty's Declaration of Abdication Act, 1936.

While this procedure was going on in the House of Commons a more decorous sitting of the House of Lords was progressing. In the absence of Lord Hailsham, the Lord Chancellor, the Earl of Onslow was seated on the Woolsack.

At 3.45 the Lord Privy Seal, Viscount Halifax— better known to the world as Lord Irwin—rose and read the King's Message, which at that precise moment the Speaker was reading to the crowded Commons. The formal reading over, he proceeded to voice the sentiments of the Government, of which he was the representative in the House of Lords.

Viscount Halifax said :

131

"I suppose that the feeling which is uppermost in the minds of all the people of this country, as in all parts of His Majesty's Empire, is one of bewilderment at the suddenness of the loss we have sustained, together with a deepening sense of sorrow as we come to realize its full significance. It is not difficult to appreciate how stern must have been the contest for His Majesty between conflicting loyalties. To few indeed is it given to be immune from such interior civil war ; but for none surely can the burden of decision in the solitary sphere of conscience have been so sorely weighted by the knowledge of its inevitable impact upon the life of the whole Common-wealth of which the man who had to make decision was also Sovereign head.

"It is no part of His subjects' duty, even if their hearts allowed, to pass judgment upon the conclusion which His Majesty has felt impelled to reach. We can but signify our profound emotion at the outcome of these days and weeks of painful stress, and give, if we may, a humble assurance of how close our thoughts are to those of his family who stand nearest to the King, and especially to Her for whom the noble Marquess spoke the feeling of the whole House on Tuesday.

"Your Lordships will recall the universal sense of public and of personal deprivation that followed the death of His Late Majesty, and how all who owed allegiance to the British Crown sought comfort in the promise of the new reign then begun. We knew and we have valued all that His Majesty had it in his power to give by way of inspiration, encouragement and understanding, and it is with great sadness that we have learnt of the untimely withdrawal of these gifts from the service of the State. Your Lordships will neither expect nor wish me to say more. We are yet too close to the unhappy sequence of events that has so suddenly overwhelmed both those early antici-pations and our hopes."

Lord Snell then spoke for the Labour Opposition :

"My Lords, you will have heard the statement which has been made to the House with sorrow and with deep regret. All of us had hoped that the appeals which had been made to His Majesty would have induced him to reach a different conclusion. It seems only a few short days since Edward VIII ascended the Throne amid the heartfelt greetings of his people. There is not one of us who did not wish for him a long, a happy, and a prosperous reign, and none of us would have withheld from him co-operation in any effort necessary for the good of our nation and of His Majesty's personal happiness and well-being. To-day we have a different and melancholy situation to face. By his own will, and against the earnest solicitations, many times repeated, of his responsible advisers, His Majesty has decided to take this momentous step. We can only, with infinite regret, accept his decision. He is the master of his own destiny, and he has made his choice. This is not the occasion when any criticism of the issues in this grievous matter could usefully be made. Our thoughts and feelings are so deeply concerned with the personal sorrow of parting with and from a Ruler whose career and promise some of us have followed with hope and satisfaction since his birth, that other matters seem inappropriate.

"I am certainly not in a position to speak concerning the facts, because I do not know them. Less, perhaps, than any of your Lordships, can we on these Benches venture upon an interpretation of the King's mind. We know him only in his official capacity, and we have had no closer contact with him than has been enjoyed by the general public. We do not complain of that, but it does lessen the opportunity to offer to him understanding assistance at this, the great crisis of his life. I hope your Lordships will agree that in a position of unusual difficulty and without the information which has been available to the Government, my own Party has tried to face this tragic situation with a becoming dignity and restraint. Now that the deciding step is taken, and we are called upon to accept the Abdication of a King to whom we were bound by many precious experiences and memories, it only remains to us to think of him as in happier days and to express our deep sympathy with him in the difficult issues that he had to face. Members of my own Party have special reasons of sorrow at his departing. As a Prince he was sympathetic and progressively-minded, and as a King he showed great interest in the well-being of the poorer sections of his people. His sympathy with the miners in the hour of their great need and his more recent and courageously-expressed sympathy with the unemployed workers in the Distressed Areas make this occasion for us one of special sorrow and regret.

"There is nothing more to be said. We must accept a situation which we have not made and which we cannot influence. And yet there remains two things that I must say—first, to express our sympathy with the Prime Minister who has had both long and arduous and most difficult duties to perform. In my opinion, with such facts as are at my disposal, he sought to be a good friend to the King and to fulfil at the same time his duty to the nation and Empire which his position as Prime Minister imposed upon him. The second thing I must do is, on behalf of my noble friends, to express our very sincere sympathy with Queen Mary and with all the members of her family. May I venture to hope that Her Majesty will be comforted at this hour by the constant and affectionate goodwill of the people of the British nation and the peoples of the British Commonwealth and Empire. Our minds inevitably and anxiously turn to the problems of the immediate future. Certain consequential decisions will be required following what we do here to-day, and some of them will require the careful consideration of Parliament."

After a short debate the House of Lords adjourned. Only some hundred members had been present. Many of the remainder had been crowded in the inner lobby or seated in the Peers' gallery to hear Mr. Baldwin make his historic statement in the House of Commons.

As far as Parliament was concerned, except for formalities, the crisis was now over. The problem which had held the world's attention for a week had been resolved. Evening papers carried the day's proceedings into the streets where the public besieged the sellers and greedily devoured the news.

Queen Mary, who was at the home of the

Duke of York when the announcement of the King's abdication was made in Parliament, was wildly cheered by the crowds as she left. There were a few minor demonstrations outside the Palace and in Whitehall, but on the whole the public took the matter calmly and, indeed, with relief.

That night the Duke of York—whose photographs had been featured prominently in the evening papers as his brother's successor—dined with the King at Fort Belvedere.

The B.B.C. announced in the evening that King Edward would broadcast "as a private person" the next day at 10 p.m.

Chapter IX

THE CRISIS IS RESOLVED

THE HOUSE OF COMMONS GATHERED
in good numbers at eleven o'clock on Friday
morning, December 11, to pass the Abdication
Bill. When Mr. Baldwin entered he was again
cheered. In moving the Second Reading of the
Bill the Prime Minister said :

"The provisions of this Bill require very few
words of explanation. It is a matter which, of
course, concerns the Dominions and their Con-
stitutions, just as it concerns us. As the House
will see, four Dominions—Canada, Australia,
New Zealand and South Africa—have desired
to be associated with this Bill. As regards the
Irish Free State, I received a message from
Mr. De Valera yesterday telling me that he

proposed to call his Parliament together to-day to pass legislation dealing with the situation in the Irish Free State.

"The legal and constitutional position is somewhat complex, and any points with regard to it which anyone desires to raise would more properly be dealt with at a later stage.

"The Bill gives effect to His Majesty's Abdication, and provides that His Royal Highness the Duke of York shall succeed to the Throne in the same way, and with the same results as if the previous reign had ended in the ordinary course. It is necessary to have an Act of Parliament because the succession to the Throne is governed by the Act of Settlement, which makes no provision for an abdication or for a succession consequent upon an abdication. It is also necessary expressly to amend that Act by eliminating His Majesty, and his issue and descendants from the succession. This is effected by Sub-sections (1) and (2) of Clause 1.

"Sub-section (3) deals with the Royal Marriages Act, 1772. This Act provides, in effect, that no descendants of George II, other than the issue of princesses married into foreign families, shall be capable of contracting a marriage without the consent of the King, with the proviso that where that consent is refused in the case of such a descendant above the age of 25, he may give

wealth, and in the interests of this country, we should see the utmost simplicity in the monarchy, which will, I believe, bind together people and Monarch more closely than before."

Followed an hour and a half's discussion on an amendment moved by Mr. Maxton and seconded by Mr. Campbell Stephen, supported by Mr. Gallacher and Mr. G. D. Hardie, all of whom expressed the general dissent indicated in their speeches of the preceding day. The amendment read :

"To leave out the word 'That' to the end of the question, and to insert instead thereof :

"This House declines to give a second reading to a Bill which has been necessitated by circumstances which show clearly the danger to this country and to the British Commonwealth of Nations inherent in an hereditary monarchy, at a time when the peace and prosperity of the people require a more stable and efficient form of government of a republican kind, in close contact with, and more responsive to, the will of the mass of the people, and which fails to give effect to the principle of popular election."

This amendment brought Sir John Simon, the Home Secretary, to his feet. Spectators knew that he had played a great part in the negotiations behind the scenes, and they listened eagerly to his first parliamentary contribution. Sir John said :

"I shall best interpret the general feeling of the House if I do not attempt to deal at any length with this manuscript Amendment. It expresses a sentiment which rouses very deep feelings of resentment in the hearts of most of us, but the conditions are such that it can be discussed calmly and, I hope, with dignity, and certainly briefly.

"It is a measure of the misfortune of all this business that it should give occasion for such an Amendment. It is true that what has happened has deeply, even inexpressibly, shocked the British people—I do not mean merely the events of yesterday, but the incidents and rumours which led up to the events of yesterday. It is right that this should be so, but the fact that it is so only demonstrates how deeply this conception of constitutional Kingship is embedded in our hearts. If it did not represent an idea deeply cherished and profoundly respected, we should care much less about what has happened than we do.

"The institution of the Throne is greater, far greater, than the life or experiences of any individual. If institutions were not greater than our frailty or the inscrutable promptings of an individual human heart, orderly development would be impossible. The hon. Member for Bridgeton (Mr. Maxton) described constitutional Monarchy as a device. Is not the Presidency of a Republic a device? History does not show that Republicanism is a guarantee of stability—certainly not of stability combined with civil liberty.

"This conception, created by the genius of the British people and valued as the symbol of Commonwealth unity, can withstand this shock, grievous though it be, and will, I believe, be once again vindicated and strengthened in the new reign. The hon. Member for Bridgeton mistakes a most grievous incident in the history of an institution for the breakdown of the institution itself. The hon. Member for Camlachie (Mr. Stephen) said just now that he supported this Amendment because he desired the will of the people to prevail. The will of the people will prevail, and when this Bill passes to-night, the individual who ascends the Throne is one who has already won our esteem and who, with his wife at his side, will hold in trust for us this precious possession."

When the members trooped into the lobbies the amendment was defeated and the Second reading was carried by 403 votes to 5.

The Committee stage was then reached and the Bill went through without much further discussion. Then Mr. Baldwin rose to move that the Bill be read a Third time. He said :

"I rise once more to-day, and only for a very few moments. I do not want this Bill to leave the House without making the few observations which I propose to make. This is the last Bill that will be presented for the Royal Assent during the present reign. The Royal Assent given to this Bill will be the last act of his present Majesty, and I should not like the Bill to go to another place without putting on record what, I feel sure, will be the feeling of this House and of the country that, though we have this duty to perform to-day, and though we are performing it with unanimity, we can never be unconscious of, and we shall always remember with regard and affection, the whole-hearted and loyal service that His Majesty has given to this country as Prince of Wales, and during the short time he has been on the Throne. Like many of his generation, he was flung into the War as a very young man, and he has served us well in trying to qualify himself for that office which he knew must be his if he lived. For all that work I should like to put on record here to-day that we are grateful and that we shall not forget. There is no need on this Bill to say anything of the future. It deals with the fate of him who is still King, and who will cease to be King in a few short hours. I felt that I could hardly reconcile it with my conscience or my feelings if I let this Bill go to another place without saying just these few words."

The Third reading was taken without a division, and the House was suspended at 12.40 p.m. and the Bill went to the Lords. At 1.52 p.m. the Speaker, who had resumed the Chair at 1.41, reported that the Royal Assent had been given to the Bill. At 1.55 the Prime Minister rose to state that an Accession Council would meet on the morning of December 12th "to approve the Proclamation to proclaim King George VI."

King Edward's last and King George's first Court Circular was issued.

Buckingham Palace. December 11.

"The Royal Assent was given at 1.52 p.m. to-day to His Majesty's Declaration of Abdication Bill."

"145 *Piccadilly. December* 11.

"The Right Hon. Stanley Baldwin, M.P., Prime Minister and First Lord of the Treasury, had an audience of the King this afternoon."

Later in the day Queen Mary addressed a message from Marlborough House :

"To the People of this Nation and Empire.

"I have been so deeply touched by the sympathy which has surrounded me at this time of anxiety that I must send a message of gratitude from the depth of my heart.

"The sympathy and affection which sustained me in my great sorrow less than a year ago have not failed me now, and are once again my strength and stay.

"I need not speak to you of the distress which fills a mother's heart when I think that my dear son has deemed it to be his duty to lay down his charge, and that the reign which had begun with so much hope and promise has so suddenly ended.

"I know that you will realize what it has cost him to come to this decision ; and that, remembering the years in which he tried so eagerly to serve and help his country and Empire, you will ever keep a grateful remembrance of him in your hearts.

"I commend to you his brother, summoned so unexpectedly and in circumstances so painful, to take his place. I ask you to give to him the same full measure of generous loyalty which you gave to my beloved husband, and which you would willingly have continued to give to his brother.

"With him I commend my dear daughter-in-law, who will be his Queen. May she receive the same unfailing affection and trust which you have given to me for six and twenty years. I know that you have already taken her children to your hearts.

"It is my earnest prayer that in spite of, nay through, this present trouble, the loyalty and unity of our land and Empire may by God's blessing be maintained and strengthened. May He bless and keep and guide you always.

"MARY R."

The Archbishops of Canterbury and York issued a joint statement concerning prayers for the King and the Royal Family. In this statement, Queen Mary is spoken of as "the Queen Mother". It reads :

"Incumbents and all who use the Book of Common Prayer on Sunday next, the first Sunday of a new reign, will desire some guidance as to the form of prayer for the King and the Royal Family.

"Pending the customary formal order, which will be published in due course, we authorize the following changes—namely, for the word 'Edward' wherever it occurs the substitution of the word 'George', and for the words 'our gracious Queen Mary, Albert Duke of York, the Duchess of York and all the Royal Family' the substitution of the words 'our gracious Queen Elizabeth, Mary the Queen Mother, the Princess Elizabeth, and all the Royal Family'."

In the Dominions steps were taken to pass complementary measures arising out of the Abdication*.

---

* All the Dominions, except the Irish Free State gave their prompt assent to the Abdication Bill. Formal legislation may be necessary later. Mr. Eamon De Valera took the opportunity to make important alterations in the Free State Constitution, and rushed them through the Dail in two days. As it was, the Irish Free State acknowledged King Edward as King for a day longer than any other part of the British Commonwealth. These alterations in the Constitution remove the name of the King from all the internal concerns of the Free State, but retain it for external affairs, the King being recognized as the "symbol of co-operation", of the Dominions in the Commonwealth. By this act the Irish Free State does not leave the Commonwealth although, so far as internal affairs are concerned, she has assumed what is, in effect, a Republican form of government. This curious state of affairs arose out of the Constitution (Amendment No. 27) Bill being too hastily prepared.

The world was now anxiously waiting for the valedictory message of the late King to the nation. Almost every country had made arrangements to relay the speech, which was to be broadcast from a room in the Augusta Tower of Windsor Castle. Cinemas and theatres interrupted their programmes to give their patrons the opportunity to listen to the speech.

Ten o'clock arrived. Sir John Reith, Director-General of the B.B.C., announced :

"This is Windsor Castle. His Royal Highness Prince Edward."

Tense listeners heard a door close. Then in the well-known voice he began his last message to the peoples he had served :

"At long last I am able to say a few words of my own.

"I have never wanted to withhold anything, but until now it has not been constitutionally possible for me to speak.

"A few hours ago I discharged my last duty as King and Emperor, and now that I have been succeeded by my brother, the Duke of York, my first words must be to declare my allegiance to him.

"This I do with all my heart.

"You all know the reasons which have impelled me to renounce the Throne, but I want you to understand that in making up my mind I did not forget the country or the Empire, which as Prince of Wales and lately as King I have for 25 years tried to serve.

"But you must believe me when I tell you that I have found it impossible to carry the heavy burden of responsibility and discharge my duties as King as I would wish to do without the help and support of the woman I love.

"And I want you to know that the decision I have made has been mine and mine alone. This was a thing I had to judge entirely for myself. The other person most nearly concerned has tried up to the last to persuade me to take a different course.

"I have made this, the most serious decision of my life, only upon a single thought—of what would in the end be best for all.

"This decision has been made less difficult to me by the sheer knowledge that my brother, with his long training in the public affairs of this country and with his fine qualities, will be able to take my place forthwith without interruption or injury to the life and progress of the Empire.

"And he has one matchless blessing, enjoyed by so many of you, and not bestowed on me, a happy home with his wife and children.

"During these hard days I have been comforted by Her Majesty, my mother, and by my family. The Ministers of the Crown, and in particular Mr. Baldwin, the Prime Minister, have always treated me with full consideration. There has never been any constitutional difference between me and them, and between me and Parliament.

"Bred in the constitutional traditions by my father, I should never have allowed any such issue to arise. Ever since I was Prince of Wales, and later on when I occupied the Throne, I have been treated with the greatest kindness by all classes of people, wherever I have lived or journeyed throughout the Empire. For that I am very grateful.

"I now quit altogether public affairs, and I lay down my burden. It may be some time before I return to my native land, but I shall always follow the fortunes of the British race and Empire with profound interest, and if at any time in the future I can be found of service to His Majesty in a private station I shall not fail.

"And now we all have a new King. I wish

him and you, his people, happiness and prosperity with all my heart.   God bless you all.   GOD SAVE THE KING !"

A moment later all the B.B.C. transmitters closed down.

Chapter X

GEORGE VI PROCLAIMED

KING GEORGE VI ATTENDED A MEETING of the Accession Council at St. James' Palace at 11 a.m. on Saturday, December 12th, and took the Accession Oath. He also made a declaration to the Accession Council :

"Your Royal Highnesses, My Lords, and Gentlemen,

"I meet you to-day in circumstances which are without parallel in the history of the country. Now that the duties of sovereignty have fallen to me I declare to you my adherence to the strict principles of constitutional government and my resolve to work before all else for the welfare of the British Commonwealth of Nations.

154

"With my wife as helpmeet by my side I take up the heavy task which lies before me. In it I look for all the support of all my peoples.

"Furthermore, my first act on succeeding my brother will be to confer on him a dukedom, and he will henceforth be known as his Royal Highness the Duke of Windsor."

At three o'clock that afternoon the new King and his family watched the Proclamation ceremony in London from a window in Marlborough House. Queen Elizabeth, who was suffering from a mild attack of influenza, remained at 145, Piccadilly.

The age-old ritual of proclaiming the new Monarch by the Gentlemen at Arms, at Charing Cross, the Temple and the Royal Exchange, was observed. The B.B.C. broadcast the ceremony at St. James' Palace, where the Garter-King at Arms, Sir Gerald Wollaston, read the Proclamation. Then, after a broadcast of the Royal Salute in Hyde Park, listeners were switched over to hear Mr. Mackenzie King, Canadian Premier, proclaim the new Ruler in Ottawa.

After leaving St. James's Palace, King George VI returned to Buckingham Palace, where he received in audience Sir John Simon and Mr. J. Ramsay MacDonald, and announced that the date of the Coronation would be May 12th, 1937, the date originally fixed for the coronation of Edward VIII.

Later that afternoon it was learned that the Duke of Windsor had disembarked from the *Fury* at Boulogne and had boarded a train bound for Austria.

Before the broadcast from Windsor Castle the former King dined with the new King, Queen Mary, the Duke of Gloucester and the Princess Royal at the Royal Lodge, Windsor Park. When the broadcast was over he entered his car and took the road to Portsmouth, where he boarded the waiting destroyer.

It was a dark night. A thick fog had settled on the Channel and was driving inland as the car raced through the silent country lanes, past quiet houses wherein people still sat wondering at the drama of that valedictory message of their late Monarch. Behind the car came two more cars, acting as escort. In Portsmouth they took the wrong road and had to be directed to the Unicorn Gate of the Docks.

The cars arrived at about 12.30, and the Duke went to the house of Admiral Fisher before proceeding to the destroyer. When he and his small party were on board, the *Fury* slipped away into the fog, bound for Boulogne. For hours the boat lay at anchor, waiting for the appropriate time when it might slip into Boulogne harbour so that the Duke could board the train. The Duke was accompanied by his Equerry, Colonel Piers Legh, and his personal detective, Chief Inspector David Storrier. With the party was the Duke's favourite Cairn terrier.

After a brief ceremony of welcome, the party entered the train and began their cross-country journey to Castle Enzesfeld, the home of Baron Eugene de Rothschild, grandson of the British-born Baroness Alfonse de Rothschild, and head of the Paris house.

Into the train scrambled scores of journalists and cameramen. At each stop *en route* they leaped from the train, hoping to catch a glimpse of the Duke, but only to see a railway servant exercising the terrier.

As the train drew into Vienna a cordon of police formed round the special car, and allowed no one to approach it. Inside the cordon a number of Viennese officials and the British Minister in Vienna, Sir Walford Selby, stood to receive the Duke. He might have been hurried away, but with characteristic generosity he suggested that the photographers be allowed to get some pictures.

"I want you to let the photographers come along," he said. "They have had a very tough journey and they deserve some results. Let's turn back."

For five minutes he submitted to the attentions of the photographers, then entered a car, drove swiftly through the well-guarded and wintry countryside to Castle Enzesfeld, twenty-five miles south of Vienna.

The crisis had now passed into the long and chequered annals of the English Crown. On Sunday evening, December 13, 1936, the Archbishop of Canterbury, in a broadcast sermon said :

"It is right to be proud of the way in which the nation has stood the test. Yet let there be no boasting in our pride. Rather let it pass into humble and reverent thankfulness for this renewed token of the guidance of the nation's life by the overruling providence of our God.

"What pathos, nay, what tragedy, surrounds the central figure of these swiftly moving scenes. On the 11th day of December 248 years ago King James II fled from Whitehall. By a strange coincidence on the 11th day of December last week, King Edward VIII, after speaking his last words to his people, left Windsor Castle, the centre of all the splendid traditions of his ancestors, and his Throne, and went out an exile. In the darkness he left these shores.

"Seldom, if ever, has any British Sovereign come to the Throne with greater natural gifts for his kingship. Seldom, if ever, has any Sovereign been welcomed by a more enthusiastic loyalty. From God he had received a high and sacred trust. Yet by his own will he has abdicated—he has surrendered the trust. With characteristic frankness he has told us his motive. It was a craving for private happiness.

"Strange and sad it must be that for such a motive, however strongly it pressed upon his heart, he should have disappointed hopes so high and abandoned a trust so great. Even more strange and sad it is that he should have sought his happiness in a manner inconsistent with Christian principles of marriage, and within a social circle whose standards and ways of life are alien to all the best instincts and traditions of his people.

"Let those who belong to this circle know that to-day they stand rebuked by the judgment of the nation who had loved King Edward.

"I have shrunk from saying these words. But I have felt compelled for the sake of sincerity and truth to say them.

"Yet for one who has known him since his childhood, who has felt his charm and admired his gifts, these words cannot be the last. How can we forget the high hopes and promise of his youth, his most genuine care for the poor, the suffering of the unemployed, his years of eager service both at home and across the seas ? It is the remembrance of these things that wrings from our heart the cry : 'The pity of it, O the pity of it !' To the infinite mercy and the protecting care of God we commit him now, wherever he may be.

"There are two other figures who will always stand out among the memories of these fateful days. One is our ever-honoured and beloved Queen Mary. During all the strain of tense anxiety, deep as her distress has been, her wonderful calmness, self-control, steadiness of judgment have never failed.

"The thought of her reign by the side of her beloved husband for twenty-five years, of the sorrow which came to her when he passed from her sight, and of the fresh sorrow which within less than a year she has had to bear, is a three-fold cord which binds her fast to the hearts of her people.

"The other person who has earned our gratitude and admiration is the Prime Minister. With great courage he took the whole burden on himself. As one to whom throughout all these anxieties he has given his confidence, I can personally testify that he has combined, as perhaps he only could, the constitutional responsibility of a Minister with the understanding of a man and the faithfulness of a friend. History will record that he was the pilot who, by God's help, steered the ship of State through difficult currents, through dangerous rocks and shoals, into the harbour where now it safely rests.

"It is this whole-hearted loyalty which with one heart and voice the peoples of this realm and Empire offer him to-day. He will prove worthy of it.

"In manner and speech he is more quiet and reserved than his brother, and here may I add a parenthesis which may not be unhelpful. When his people listen to him they will note an occasional and momentary hesitation in his speech. But he has brought it into full control, and to those who hear it need cause no sort of embarrassment, for it causes none to him who speaks.

"He is frank, straightforward, unaffected. The six thousand boys from our public schools and from the homes of working folk whom for the last fifteen years he has gathered in the comradeship of a summer camp know that he has been himself a boy among them. In varied fields of service, in the Navy, in the Air Force, in association with all manner of public and charitable causes, he has gained a wide experience. He has made the welfare of industrial workers his special care and study. There is no branch of industry where he is not at home. In his visits with the Queen to Central Africa, to Australia and New Zealand he has studied the peoples and the problems of the great Empire over which he is now called to rule. He has high ideals of life and duty, and he will pursue them with a quiet steadfastness of will. He inherits the name ; he will follow the example of King George V, to whose memory let us offer now the homage of our undying affection and respect.

"No passage in the last message of the Duke of Windsor, as we must now learn to call our late King, was more touching than that in which he spoke of his brother's 'matchless blessing—a happy home with wife and children.' King George will have at his side the gentle strength and quiet wisdom of a wife who has already endeared herself to all by her grace, her charm, her bright and eager kindliness of heart.

"As for her dear children, I will only say that they are as delightful and fascinating as she was in her own childhood as I remember it over thirty years ago. Truly it is good to think that among all the homes of the Empire—the homes from which all that is best within it springs—none can be more happy and united that the home of our King and Queen.

"A King has gone. God be with him. A King has come. God bless him, keep him, guide him, now and ever.

"We are all rallying to our new King. Will there not be a rally also to the King of Kings? We still call ourselves a Christian nation. But if title is to be a reality and not a mere phrase there must be a renewal in our midst of definite and deliberate allegiance to Christ—to His standards of life, to the principles of His kingdom.

"We are now able to look forward with hope and joy to the Coronation of our King. He himself and his kingship will then be solemnly consecrated to the service of the most high God. But the august ceremony will be bereft of a great part of its true meaning unless it is accompanied by a new consecration of his people to the same high service. So may King and people alike acknowledge their allegiance to God and dedicate themselves to seek first His kingdom and His righteousness."

Thus spake the Archbishop of Canterbury. It remains, however, for history to pronounce its judgment on Edward VIII.

The crisis had opened with the protest of the Bishop of Bradford, and it closed with the broadcast sermon of the Primate. A King had gone, but the Throne remained ; and out of the welter of conflicting events emerged the Prime Minister, Stanley Baldwin, who had successfully carried through the role of a modern Cromwell.